The Reality

by Lola Morrison

Orla Kelly Publishing
Kilbrody,
Mount Oval,
Rochestown,
Cork,
Ireland

Contents

Foreword

The one adage that I disagree with is 'Money is the root of all evil'. Money is a reality of life. I cannot remember the last time I tried to buy groceries in exchange for pebbles or a freshly shot piece of venison.

In my experience of witnessing financial crime and having been a victim of fraud myself, greed is the root of all evil.

I am amazed at the number of people who worship money but have simply decided that they do not want to earn it honourably. What with everything from the increase in phony insurance claims to sophisticated scams targeting senior citizens' pension savings, I do wonder what has happened to the moral fabric of our society.

Unfortunately for the honest members of society, we incur the cost of fraud. Surprisingly, when a judge and jury convict and sentence these criminals, they are usually aghast at the punishment they receive. With that said, I do hope the following publication helps to raise your awareness about fraud.

Acknowledgements

This publication is primarily for Continuing Professional Development (CPD) purposes. The contents are based on my opinion, private education, independent research, and interactions with people from all levels of society. I tried to give acknowledgment wherever possible and this publication is not a substitute for any legal advice or professional services.

I am delighted that the Association of Certified Fraud Examiners (ACFE) granted me permission to use data, statistics, and information from its biennial Report to the Nations.

I donate to Wikipedia and I am sincerely grateful to all the volunteers who provide free access to information.

I am incredibly appreciative of my dear friend Mrs. Bridget W for encouraging me every step of the way.

Finally, thank you to the associate from The Chartered Institute of Management Accountants (contact ID: 1-HHYB), the Certified Professional Forensic Accountant (registration number 3674) from The Institute of Certified Forensic Accountants, the holder of a Diploma in Forensic Accounting from Brentwood Open Learning College (certificate number 50856911) and the student from The Insurance Institute of America (ID: 999021494).

Of course, this publication would not be possible without the support of Orla Kelly and her team at Orla Kelly Publishing. Orla's outstanding professionalism, sound and wise advice coupled with an enthusiastic sense of humour cheered me to the finish line.

"The more extensive a man's knowledge of what has been done, the greater will be his power of knowing what to do".
Benjamin Disraeli (1804-1881)

Chapter 1

What is Fraud?

Fraud is wrongful or criminal deception intended to result in financial or personal gain. Mr. Donald R. Cressey (1919-1987) was an American criminologist and we often consider him to be the founder of the modern-day study of organised crime. Mr. Cressey developed a theory, known as the fraud triangle. He stipulated that the following three factors must exist for an individual to commit fraud:

a. Pressure and Incentive

b. Opportunity

c. Attitude and Rationalisation

Pressure and incentive include financial, personal and work-related reasons for example the pressure to pay bills, repay a high debt, fund a substance abuse problem or is simply a disgruntled employee who feels overworked, underpaid and has little respect for his employer and/or management team.

People in important levels of organisations often have more **opportunity** to commit fraud especially if there are poor or non-existent controls. In 2002, the United States of America (U.S.) Congress enacted the Sarbanes-Oxley Act (SOX Act) in response to the accounting scandals at Enron, WorldCom, and Tyco to tackle the problem of senior-level company officers committing fraud. This federal law act governs corporate responsibilities and serves to protect investors, employees, and the thousands of hard-working individuals with retirement savings and pensions invested in public companies. The SOX Act also forbids retaliation against whistle-blowers who have some connection to publicly traded companies. A whistle-blower informs an authority about something illegal happening within a company or organization.

Fraudsters often **rationalise** their behaviour and expect to repay the money at some stage in the future. Employees may also have issues with the ethics of top management and merely decide to steal from their employer and/or its clients.

What skills are most important to the successful practice of forensic accounting?

Forensic Accounting integrates accounting, auditing, and investigative skills to detect financial fraud and prevent fraudulent accounting practices in the future.

There are several skills or knowledge bases required for the forensic accountant. The following is a list of important skills:

The forensic accountant should possess good written and verbal communication skills, technical accounting knowledge including General Accepted Accounting Principles (GAAP) familiarity, auditing and/or industry experience, be tech savvy, and have sound legal knowledge.

They should also have good investigation skills and observe the chain of custody when gathering evidence. The chain of custody, also known as the chain of evidence, is the movement and location of physical evidence from the time it is obtained until the time it is presented in court.

They should possess the ability to objectively analyse and evaluate an issue to form judgement, which is also known as critical thinking, and having sound business knowledge is also highly desirable.

What qualities of mind and/or body should a forensic accountant possess?

The forensic accountant should have excellent interpersonal skills, as they are often involved with interviewing suspects who may be high ranking officers of companies. They usually deal with people from all levels of society, e.g. police officers, lawyers, court officials, and jurors, amongst many others. They should co-operate with and respect their colleagues which can be a large team of people. Furthermore, they must be methodical in their work, have common sense, and display a calm demeanour. It helps if they can think like a fraudster as the old saying goes: "You have to think like a thief to catch a thief." Intelligence and confidence are also desirable qualities, as well as flexibility and resilience in the face of adversity. The most important trait, in my opinion, is the need to be highly analytical. Analytical skills are the ability to visualise, gather information, articulate, analyse, solve complex problems, and make decisions.

What are the basic steps involved in a fraud investigation?

The steps are as follows:

1. **Accepting the investigation**

   The investigation team must have the knowledge and experience to accept the case. Forensic accounting is highly specialised and requires formal training, including the handling and safe keeping of evidence. There should be no conflict of interest, especially if authorities approach an accounting firm that audits the company where the suspected fraud has taken place.

2. **Planning the investigation**

   The investigation team must carefully plan their approach and determine the objectives of their assignment. These objectives include determining the type of fraud committed, how long the fraud occurred, and how the suspects concealed the alleged fraud. They need to identify everyone involved in the fraud and determine the monetary loss to the company, gather the necessary evidence, present their findings in court, and recommend fraud prevention techniques going forward.

3. **Gathering Evidence**

   This includes account reconciliations, document reviews, analysing, and identifying gaps in internal control, comparing trends over time to identify any patterns of misappropriation, identifying time and location of computer data alterations using computer assisted auditing techniques (CAAT), and carrying out interviews and/or discussions with staff.

4. Reporting

The investigation team can expect to prepare a report for the company advising them of the evidence obtained, the amount of financial damage caused by the alleged fraud, the company's internal control weaknesses, and how the fraudsters committed the act. They may also need to document recommendations for improving internal controls.

5. Court Proceedings

The investigation usually leads to a court case and the forensic accountant may need to present evidence in court. They often need to explain evidence in plain language, as many of the people present will be non-accounting people. Forensic accountants should be able to defend their conclusions.

What is the difference between financial auditing and forensic accounting?

Financial auditing is different from forensic accounting in the following areas:

Financial Auditing is a continual service that evaluates the compliance of financial information with regulatory standards usually for public companies by an external independent entity and complying with efficient market theory. We can define efficient market theory as the expected return on an investor's financial commitment according to their perceived risk at the time of investment. Financial auditors use sampling and materiality to gain a sense of comfort with the numbers and they produce financial statements, management letters, and auditor reports.

Forensic Accounting serves to prove or disprove fraud in a business in a risk prone environment or when someone suspects or reports a fraud. Forensic accountants provide analytical accounting and financial information to support legal and administrative decisions. The reporting is also quite different from financial auditing as forensic accountants often produce investigation and/or expert reports.

Case Study

Adam is the executive officer of a school in a small town and has ultimate authority for all items payable from the school's annual budget. In his position, he travels to education conventions and meetings in various cities across the country. Although Adam is an excellent accountant and the day-to-day affairs of the school run smoothly, his difficult personality does not engage the school's Board of Directors (The Board). This affected his attempts to gain approval for his proposals. Frustrated and increasingly resentful, Adam sought revenge by using his signing authority to approve personal expenditures and write cheques to himself. He used the school's credit card to pay for fuel and repairs to his private car. He also submitted and approved bills for personal meals and entertainment on weekends. His secretary blew the whistle on him when she became aware of some of these activities.

Considering the above situation, let us look at the following questions. Please keep in mind that the school's Board of Directors assigned the power of administration of the school's property in trust to Adam and his legal obligation is to administer it solely for these purposes.

1. **How should we start the investigation for the above case?**

   Initially we should determine what type of fraud was committed. In this instance, it is conflict of interest. This falls under the category of corruption as Adam used his signing authority to con the school out of money for many items of small and large monetary value. We must also figure out who is involved. We already identified Adam as the suspect and his secretary was the whistle-blower but what about the board members – were any of them involved? There seems to be a lack of control, and we must remember that the stakeholders of the school elect the Board of Directors to oversee Adam and his duties. A sample list of questions includes: What controls were in place relating to the segregation of duties? Was there any process for reviewing Adam's expenses by the board? Another important question is: Was any Board member in collusion with Adam?

2. **Which documents can help us to disclose Adam's fraudulent activities?**

   In most cases, the secretary would keep all receipts and invoices submitted by Adam for a specified period; in many companies the retention period is 5-7 years. These receipts are evidence. The investigation team needs to safeguard this evidence to prevent Adam and/or any other possible suspect from destroying it. Furthermore, the investigation team must observe the chain of evidence. As previously mentioned, this is the movement and location of physical evidence from the time they obtain it until they present it in court.

3. **If we need to hire a forensic accountant, what do we need to consider?**

Firstly, we need to determine if the forensic accountant has the required knowledge and experience to undertake this investigation. Forensic accountants are highly specialised so they should have most of the characteristics one would expect from a qualified forensic accountant and please note that the forensic accountant also needs to accept the investigation. As per the case study, it is a small city so a conflict of interest may exist. Ideally, we should hire a firm from another town or county.

4. **Should we interview Adam? If so, at which stage?**

Yes, we must interview Adam numerous times. Once the investigation team produces enough evidence, we should conduct the initial interview with Adam. This is a crucial interview as he may confess to his crime during this discussion. He may also lie, and it is important to record this interview. Experience has shown that many guilty suspects change their story many times before they appear before a judge and jury in court proceedings.

Corruption is simply crime without conscience.
George Richard Marek (1902-1987)

Chapter 2

Crime and The Economy

The effect of crime on the economy is substantial. Crime influences the economy on a microeconomic and macroeconomic level. Microeconomics focuses on the effects of crime on business and individuals, while macroeconomics analyses the consequences of crime on local communities, domestic, and global markets. Crime leads to material and immaterial costs for victims, and forces local and national authorities to spend considerable amounts of money on the prevention and detection of crime in addition to the prosecution and punishment of criminals.

How does crime cost the economy and taxpayers?

The cost reality of crime locally and nationally can be enormous. The following costs affect the taxpayers:

- Operating and maintaining police departments.
- Operating and maintaining courts.
- Providing public defenders for the accused.
- Running and maintaining prisons.
- Hospitalisation and medical treatment for victims.
- Drug rehabilitation and prevention – as this is normally funded by the public purse in conjunction with the private sector.

The above also affects the economy but there are additional costs to the economy such as:

- Development of organisations to prevent the occurrence of crime community programs such as crime stoppers and neighbourhood watch associations.

- Costly court prosecutors.

- In order to offset the cost of crime, businesses commonly increase prices which affects consumers. Companies are also subject to downsizing and closing, which leads to redundancies.

- Insurance companies regularly increase policyholder premiums because of crime related claims.

What is Arson?

Arson is a criminal offence which is the malicious and intentional burning of a building. If someone breaks and enters a building, and burns it without intending to do so, they are still guilty of arson. The malicious and intentional burning of timberland, grasslands or plains also falls under arson.

There is also arson insurance fraud, whereby individuals set fire to their own properties to receive insurance money to repay loans and/or mortgages, this is especially prevalent when the properties are worth less than the balance owing on their mortgage (also known as negative equity). Insurance loss adjustors who investigate private dwelling arson often discover that the home-owners were not at home when the arson occurred and precious family pets, important legal documents, and personal valuables were absent from the property; this is often an early indication that the arson was committed or arranged by the home owners. Slight burns, smoke damage or staining of a building without any disfiguring, destruction or actual burning does not constitute arson.

What is money laundering?

Money laundering is the process of transforming the proceeds of crime and corruption into seemingly legitimate assets. Assets include tangible and intangible assets. Tangible assets have physical form such as buildings, land and intangible assets have no physical form, such as patents and other intellectual property.

Some money laundering activities include:

- Any money derived from unlawful activities.
- Using cash to purchase various properties.
- The transfer of private and public money and other monetary instruments to and from overseas or domestically.
- Depositing large amounts of money into different financial institutions and maintaining illegal offshore bank accounts with large balances.

What is 'embezzlement'? Why is it considered a financial crime?

When a member or members of staff diverts business income to one's personal use, or in other words steals business income, this is embezzlement. It is different from skimming as skimming applies to owners or officers of a company who steal from the business. Embezzlement usually occurs in cash businesses such as bars, nightclubs, and grocery stores. Tracing the money back to the culprit is difficult to prove.

In the case of embezzlement, the property does not belong to the perpetrator, and he or she steals the property for his or her own personal use or benefit. Good old-fashioned greed will entice most people to commit financial crime.

There are usually three factors seen in financial crime:

- The presence of something valuable.

- An opportunity to take something without getting caught.

- A perpetrator willing to commit an offence.

What is forgery? And what is the difference between forgery and uttering?

Forgery is falsifying a document or any writing. Uttering is passing it off as real. For example, if I unlawfully write a check from someone else's bank account and cash it, then I have committed forgery and uttering. Forgery is writing the check and uttering is cashing the check.

The intention to deceive is the basis of the crime of forgery.

The crime of forgery must have the following two features:

1. A person signed a document but he or she was not the person who should have signed.

2. Someone made the signature illegally.

If someone made a minor change to a signature that did not affect the legal liability of each party concerned, then this is not forgery.

Uttering pertains to any person who offers or publishes any forged instrument or writing and knows that it is false, and they also intend to deceive another party. On the other hand, if someone tries to pay another person using counterfeit money and genuinely does not know that the notes or coins are counterfeit, then this person is not committing uttering.

The following are specific examples of uttering or publishing:

- Presenting a fake licence as evidence to receive compensation.
- Depositing a fake cheque to a personal account.
- Delivering a forged note to pay a debt.
- Obtaining certification of a forged will.

Case Study

As part of an ongoing investigation, police officers raided a house and found a large quantity of cash. The occupants of the house claimed that the monies were savings which they had recently withdrawn from their bank accounts. The police suspected that the funds were the proceeds of the crime they were investigating and made an application to confiscate the funds.

The defendants' solicitors obtained an accountant's report which concluded that the monies had indeed come from legitimate savings. The police instructed a forensic accountant to review that report's findings. He was able to show that the couple had spent more cash than received and concluded that the husband and wife must have had access to unidentified sources of income. The couple refused to provide an explanation for the unidentified income, so the court granted an application to confiscate the monies discovered by the police.

Based on the above case, what do we think the forensic accountant would have assessed to get to know the facts about the monies? And how he was able to conclude that the husband and wife must have had access to unidentified sources of income?

Initially, the forensic accountant should review the findings in the accountant's report. I am assuming the defendant's accountant report included a set of financial statements and bank account reconciliations. The analysis of the bank accounts is particularly important in the forensic accountant's investigation. He will look at the several types of transactions, most banks record deposits, and withdrawals in distinct categories which are usually cheques, cash or transfers and identify the source of these funds if possible.

In this instance, I believe the forensic accountant would classify this financial crime as potential money laundering and investigate the following:

- Did the couple buy substantial amounts of property (both real and intangible) in their name or aliases with cash? And if so, where did they obtain this cash?

- Do they have many bank accounts domestically and internationally? What are the balances in these accounts?

When did the deposits and withdrawals take place? How much for each transaction?

- Are the couple employed and what is their annual salary?

- Do the couple have legitimate investments that generate dividends?

- Did the couple liquidate their legitimate investments and make a considerable return?

- Do the couple have legitimate properties that generate rental income?

The forensic accountant's conclusion that they derived the money from unlawful activities takes into consideration the answers to the questions above, the amount of cash recovered by the police and the presence of more cash deposits than legitimate withdrawals in their bank accounts.

The forensic accountant should also be able to name the people involved in the fraud; for example, if the accountant or the defending attorney were in collusion with the couple.

I expect that the forensic accountant in conjunction with law enforcement interviewed the accountant and questioned his findings, discussed the accountant's findings with the defendants' solicitors and hopefully was physically present in interviews conducted by law enforcement with the defendants when they were interviewed both separately and together. I also like to think the investigation team concealed the identity of the forensic accountant.

The forensic accountant should carefully follow the chain of custody as it pertains to the movement and location of physical evidence. If he or she does not follow it, the defendants may challenge the evidence or even deem it to be inadmissible in court proceedings.

The forensic accountant in this case probably wrote up his findings in a report for the police and used straightforward English language so non-accounting people could also review and understand his report. The prosecutors, police or the forensic accountant may need to present this report in court.

The fraudster's greatest liability is the certainty that the fraud is too clever to be detected.

Louis J. Freeh (American attorney and former judge)

Chapter 3

Psychology of a Fraudster

What is Occupational Fraud?

Frauds committed against any company by its own executives, directors, and employees is known as occupational fraud. It is worth noting that upon incorporation, a company is a legal entity. Therefore, it has the same rights and duties as a natural person. A company is a separate legal entity from its owners and members and can prosecute and/or be prosecuted in its own legal name.

Company shareholders appoint a Board of Directors (The Board), which in turn has ultimate governing authority over the company. In its role as trustee for the company, The Board can only use the company's property and resources for the long-term benefit of the company, and not for personal use. The Board also appoints and oversees the company's executive management team and the Chief Executive Officer (CEO) handles the daily executive management of the company according to the Board's orders and instructions.

What is the difference between high and low-level thieves?

One of the differences between high-level and low-level thieves is the severity and frequency of the thefts. In occupational fraud, high ranking managers and employees usually steal larger amounts of money (i.e. higher severity) rather than lower-level employees who usually steal lesser amounts of money but more regularly (i.e. higher frequency). Higher level employees are normally able to override and bypass internal controls, as they are often involved in reviewing or even aiding in developing organisational controls. One plausible reason for the higher occurrence of low-level thefts, is because there are more low-level employees.

Whilst there are many differences between high-level and low-level thieves, both are usually long-term employees of the company and have never been subject to criminal charges.

The Association of Certified Fraud Examiners, Inc. (The ACFE) publishes a biennial report on occupational fraud and abuse. According to its 2018 Report to the Nations, Copyright 2018 by the Association of Certified Fraud Examiners, Inc. (The 2018 RTTN), there is a correlation between a culprit's position in the company and the severity of the loss. For example: in the United States, 18% were owners or executives, 31% were managers, and 48% were employees. However, the median amount stolen by owners or executives was a whopping USD$637,000, whilst managers stole USD$150,000 and employees netted USD$50,000.

In Canada, 23% were owners or executives stealing an average of USD$600,000; 27% were managers who pocketed an average of USD$205,000 and 47% were employees taking an average of USD$156,000.

In Western Europe of those who committed fraud; 18% were owners or executives, 34% were managers, and 41% were employees. The median amount stolen by owners or executives amounted to USD$500,000, USD$235,000 by managers, and USD$90,000 by employees.

In Eastern Europe and Western/Central Asia, the 2018 RTTN noted that 28% were owners or executives and stole on average a staggering amount of USD$3,700,000. Managers accounted for 33% and pocketed an average of USD$155,000 and 39% were employees, who stole a median amount of USD$28,000.

In the Asia-Pacific region, the statistics were as follows: 26% were owners or executives and stole an average of USD$1,000,000; 41% were managers and swiped an average of USD$323,000, and 30% were employees who stole a median amount of USD$58,000.

In Sub-Sharan Africa, 14% were owners or executives who stole an average of USD$2,716,000; 36% were managers who took an average of USD$73,000, and 48% were employees who stole a median amount of USD$55,000.

NOTE: *As per the ACFE's Analysis Methodology and the calculation of percentages discussed throughout this report, they used the total number of complete and relevant responses for the question(s) being analysed. Specifically, they excluded any blank responses or instances where the participant indicated that he or she did not know the answer to a question. Consequently, the total number of cases included in each analysis varies. In addition, several survey questions allowed participants to select more than one answer. Therefore, the sum of percentages in many figures throughout the report exceeds 100%. The sum of percentages in other figures might not be exactly 100% (i.e., it might be 99% or 101%) due to rounding of individual category data.*

What is the typical profile of a white-collar criminal who tends to commit more costly occupational fraud?

Frauds involving large sums of money are committed prevalently by the following:

1. Long-term employees of an organisation.

2. High-income earners.

3. Males.

4. People aged 56 and older.

5. People with good educational backgrounds – the higher the level of education, the bigger the fraud.

6. People working in collusion with other perpetrators.

7. People who have never been subject to criminal charges.

According to the 2018 RTTN, 82% of perpetrators were male and 89% of perpetrators had no criminal history.

There is also a correlation between the length of service at a company and the frequency and severity of the loss. Employees working between six and ten years for the company committed 23% of frauds with a median loss of USD$173,000, and those employed for more than ten years committed 24% of frauds with a median loss of USD$241,000.

There is also a link between tenure and the fraudster's level of authority as those who stay with organisations for a lengthy period usually progress in the company which gives them more opportunity to commit fraud. Those aged 56 and older commit less than 9% of frauds but these cases had a median loss of USD$835,000.

Education level and seniority in the company influence the amount of stolen money. Employees with post-graduate and university degrees steal more than less educated employees causing a median loss of USD$230,000 and USD$160,000, respectively compared to fraudsters with high-school degrees or less who steal an average of USD$75,000.

Nearly half of all fraud cases involve two or more perpetrators and the average losses are far greater than those working alone.

What are 'Calculating Criminals'?

Calculating criminals normally want to compete and assert themselves. They usually have an elevated level of intelligence, are highly educated, and tend to be repeat offenders. They are predators, are inclined to take risks, have little empathy, and anxiety. They often lack inner direction, self-confidence, self-esteem, and have a powerful desire to fit in with their peers.

We are familiar with the fraud triangle which all three elements of rationalisation, opportunity, and pressure must be present for fraud to occur. In recent years, a gentleman named Jonathan T. Marks built on the fraud triangle and added two more elements, namely arrogance and competence or perceived competence, to create the 'Five Elements of the Fraud Pentagon'.

Arrogance or lack of conscious is an attitude of superiority, entitlement or greed on the part of a person who believes corporate policies simply do not apply to them. They often have large egos, think they can by-pass internal controls and will go undetected.

Many crimes are seemingly committed without economic gain but for ego, status, and sheer arrogance reasons.

Competence is an employee's ability to override internal controls and to socially control the situation to his or her advantage. Weak controls provide the opportunity to commit the fraud. Competence gives the perpetrator the opportunity to turn desire into reality.

There are six remarkably interesting common traits of personal competence:

1. Authority within an organisation.
2. Adequate intelligence to understand and exploit a situation.
3. Large egos and personal confidence.
4. Strong intimidating skills.
5. Highly devious.
6. Exceptional tolerance for stress.

What is the main difference between 'Situation Dependent Criminals' and 'Power Brokers'?

Situation Dependent Criminals are ordinary people who do not intend to harm others, but their situations drive them to commit crimes. They might think that the fraud they committed could be illegal, but it is not a crime, as they believe that they did not hurt anyone. They also convince themselves that they deserve the proceeds of their crimes because they were immaterial and meaningless however the materiality of their crimes usually increases the longer the fraud continues.

A Power Broker is a person who has influence and control in an activity. Power Brokers may have similar characteristics to both calculating criminals and situation dependent criminals. They frequently hold high positions in organisations, and they think they can obtain illegal benefits or make more money at the expense of the organisation and defraud shareholders and employers. We do not think that they started their career with this intention, but they commit their crimes for ego, status and sheer arrogance reasons, not particularly for economic gain.

What did Gwynn Nettler think about employees lying, cheating and stealing?

Criminologist Gwynn Nettler (1913-2007) authored a book called *Lying, Cheating, Stealing* (Criminal Justice Studies). According to Mr. Nettler, people are more likely to cheat if they have experienced failure in their lives, are disliked by others and have a low opinion of themselves. They are usually impulsive, distractible, impatient and selfish. Mr. Nettler also pointed out that pressure and incentive, which includes financial, personal, and work-related reasons, can lead to stealing. Those who steal and cheat regularly find it easier to continue doing it.

He also believed that factors could affect the likelihood of those who cheat. These are personal variables like core beliefs, values, and ability. There are also factors relating to the fraudster's occupation, his/her company code of ethics, the values of his/her management team and co-workers, and their company's reward system. He also mentions external factors like the economy, industry competition, and society's social values. However, Mr. Nettler thought that those who fear discovery and/or punishment, are of middle or upper social class, and are more intelligent are less likely to commit fraud.

What are the typical motivations for a white-collar criminal, which persuades them to commit fraud?

There are many reasons why people commit white-collar crime:

1. They think that they can get away with it and employees rarely face long prison sentences for white-collar crime. In addition, the organisation they work for may have no history of punishing or prosecuting people so there is no deterrent.

2. The rewards of indulging in criminal behaviour may exceed the risk of detection and apprehension. Most thieves are discovered accidentally and not by audit.

3. They believe that they need the stolen money or objects.

4. They are frustrated or dissatisfied with their job, the organisation and/or company management, and seek revenge.

5. Internal controls are very weak, and their bosses and co-workers are corrupt. This makes it easier to steal or cheat.

6. The employee is lazy or is in financial difficulty. They think it is easier to steal from the organisation than securing a second job or asking for a company loan.

7. The employee is a compulsive thief.

In the case of market downturn and if their company is facing financial challenges, these factors may influence senior executives to commit fraud, such as knowingly inflating sales. There is also an aspect of losing social status in this situation which is a significant motive for those with large egos.

How is the profile of a white-collar or blue-collar criminal different from a typical street criminal?

It is easier if we define street-crime, blue-collar crime, and white-collar crime.

Street crime is a loose term for any criminal offence in a public place. It includes robbery, purse-snatching, and thefts of a victim's private property such as smart phones.

In criminology, **blue-collar crime** is any crime committed by an individual from a lower-social class. These crimes are primarily small scale and normally provide immediate benefits for the individuals or groups involved. These crimes include the production and distribution of illegal narcotics, theft, burglary, assault or murder.

White-collar crime is a nonviolent illegal act committed by an employee or a senior manager of a company or organisation. These crimes include theft, fraud, embezzlement. White-collar crime is associated with crime committed by someone of a higher-level social class.

From the definitions above I can see some of the differences are due to the following:

Social class: White-collar criminals belong to a higher social class than blue-collar or street criminals. Street criminals are often hoodlums and repeat offenders. They frequently belong to the social underclass. The underclass is the segment of the population that occupies the lowest possible position in the social class hierarchy. Street criminals often seek immediate financial gains and usually work alone. In the case of working with others, authorities do not view it as organised crime but rather hastily loosely formed groups of individuals with the common goal of gaining illicit money through immediate criminal acts. I also think that these criminals are risk-takers and lack empathy or anxiety which is also a characteristic associated with calculating criminals.

Blue-collar crime is normally associated with the unemployed, the working class, and those holding jobs that involve low-level skills and low wages. As such, several people call criminal activities involving significant amounts of manual labour that are committed by needy defendants as Blue-Collar Crime.

White-collar crooks are from a high social class and are often intelligent and well-regarded by the public for their level of intelligence and prestige in organisations. If we take the case of the Barings Bank (Barings) scandal and the actions of Nick Leeson who caused the collapse of one of the oldest banks in the United Kingdom. This is an example of extreme greed on behalf of Leeson and the bank's ineffective internal controls. The authorities sentenced Leeson to over six years in prison, but he served less than five years. In prison, Nick Leeson authored a book called *Rogue Trader* which later became a Hollywood movie and according to latest reports, he is currently a paid keynote speaker at many events. This reinforces what some scholars describe the tolerance of white-collar crime as "a perversion of our general societal admiration for intelligence". People seem to forget the harmful effects of Leeson's actions ranging from the hundreds of millions of pounds that he gambled away and the effect on the professional and personal lives of those who worked for Barings.

I reviewed a number of documentaries concerning Leeson including 'Nick Leeson and the Fall of Barings Bank' by John Musicman, and interviews conducted by several organisations including 'Nick Leeson Interview' by Trading Thoughts and 'Interview with the Rogue Trader Nick Leeson' by Core Finance. Mr. Leeson has not taken any responsibility for his actions. To this day, I believe that Leeson continues to blame his acts of deliberate fraud on the lack of internal controls by Barings Bank, its dinosaur computer systems and his assumption that the management and staff of Barings were 'stupid' and 'bumbling fools'. Even though, Leeson could have alerted senior management at any time, he chose to continue speculating on the futures market as his eye was always on the prize of massive bonus receipts, and his fixation on being regarded as a hero of the stock markets by his peers and subordinates. During interviews, his former colleagues recalled that Leeson never wanted to be rich, just famous. Even though Leeson was under a contract of employment with Barings, he assumed that his contract of employment and the rules and regulations of the stock market simply did not apply to him.

To this present day, and in my opinion, Leeson is still arrogant and smug about his acts. He is under the impression that many members of the general public applaud him for his decimation of Barings and the fact that Dutch Bank ING eventually purchased Barings for a measly GBP£1.00.

Planning: I think we also need to take into consideration the amount of planning the criminals invest in their crimes. A typical street criminal would act instantaneously whereas blue-collar crime and especially white-collar crime take careful planning. A street criminal is a predator and usually picks his victims randomly.

If we look at blue-collar crime, a lot of it is organised crime and involves many parties or gangs that go to great length planning burglaries, drug deals, and auto theft schemes, et cetera.

White-collar crime takes a lot of planning and knowledge of systems, internal controls and identification of weaknesses, and possible loopholes. The average duration of frauds before detection for white-collar crime in the 2018 RTTN study is 16 months.

Rewards of the crime: A street criminal steals what he can. In the case of a mugging, it is usually the luck of the draw. A blue-collar criminal goes after a significant amount of money or assets and hopes to go undetected or avoid law enforcement. A white-collar criminal usually starts stealing smaller amounts of money or items, but it eventually grows in magnitude as more money and schemes are involved.

Employment status: A typical street criminal is rarely gainfully employed. Blue-collar criminals usually have employment but are involved in criminal activities to supplement their income.

White-collar criminals are employed by companies and often hold high positions in organisations, but they commit fraud for many reasons. According to the 2018 RTTN, the three most common behavioural red flags are those living beyond their means (41%), those experiencing financial difficulty (29%), and those who have unusually close relationships with vendors and/or customers (20%).

What do we think about the following quote: "Fraud is most common in organisations that have no controls, no trust, no ethical values, no profits, and no prospects"?

A company is more exposed to fraud if they have little or weak internal controls than those with tight documented controls. Controls include segregation of duties, peer or manager reviews, and employees completing control checklists as they complete their assigned tasks. It is easier to document and implement controls in SEC listed companies as they take the SOX Act seriously. Whilst some companies can go overboard on controls causing them to have a negative impact on operations, most companies review their controls from time to time and distinguish between key financial controls and those of medium or low importance.

The lack of trust between management and employees, and even between employees and co-workers, can cause angst in any company. In many instances, micro-managing undermines an employee's ability. This usually leads to frustration and anger and, as we discussed earlier, people commit fraud for revenge purposes. On the other hand, lack of communication or ineffective communication from top management can lead employees to question the company values. The employees can always argue that if they are unaware of controls then how do they know if they are doing something wrong. Nowadays a lot of legal and human resource departments publish employee policies such as a Code of Conduct and an Employee Manual that all employees must read and sign when they commence employment with a company and thereafter on an annual basis. These policies inform employees of all prohibited and punishable acts. For companies to send a clear message to employees, they need to enforce these policies uniformly across the organisation.

When management appear to lack ethical values, one of the main reasons for white-collar crimes is due to corrupt bosses setting a bad example for employees, making them more likely to steal or cheat.

Surprisingly, when the company is in a loss-making situation and there are no job prospects for the employees, fraud increases. Recently my friend's retail business was losing money. While other companies in the retail industry complained that they faced similar challenges, he could not understand why the company's financials were not improving even though he and his business partner were exerting extra effort to increase sales and reduce costs. They reduced staff and put the remaining staff on protective notice as they were seriously considering closing the business. One morning, he noticed his cashier of eight years doing something untoward. He reviewed the security cameras and noticed she was taking money from the till and putting it in her wallet. He approached her and she admitted her fraud and handed over the stolen money.

The amount represented 20% of the company's daily takings. They obviously asked her to leave and alerted law enforcement. It turns out she had a gambling addiction and she financed this addiction by stealing from her employer. The most bizarre revelation was they discovered that she started stealing larger amounts of money since management told the employees they were thinking of closing the business. She was obviously concerned that she could no longer finance her habit and decided to steal what she could while the business was still running. She is under investigation by authorities but unfortunately her employers have little recourse as she spent and gambled most of the stolen money.

What white-collar crimes that have dominated the press in recent years resulted in positive outcomes for the perpetrators?

The 2002 case involved currency trader John Rusnak who managed to incur losses of USD$691M for Allfirst bank. In 2003, authorities sentenced Mr. Rusnak to over seven years in prison. He served less than six years of his sentence. However, Mr. Rusnak has taken full responsibility for his actions, he sought help for his drug addiction, and he is bound to repay the full loss of USD$691M. Since his return to the society, Mr. Rusnak started his own business and employs those who need a purpose in life especially ex-convicts and those in drug and alcohol rehabilitation programs. He also serves as the director of unCuffed Ministries, and according to the foundation's website, "the main goal is to help youth mature, show the community how to help, and work to reduce repeat offenders".

The 2019 U.S. College Admissions fraud scandal caused quite a sensation whereby parents paid a college counselling company to alter SAT test scores to increase their children's chances of gaining admission to elite American colleges and universities. The scandal also revealed that parents bribed university coaches and administrators to falsely identify their children as talented athletes to gain acceptance into top universities. Melissa Korn, a Wall Street Journal Education Reporter, gives an excellent overview of the case online. One of the culprits namely Hollywood actor, Felicity Huffman, took full reasonability for her actions and pleaded guilty. The courts sentenced her to fourteen days in prison, one year of supervised release and 250 hours of community services. She also paid a USD$30,000 fine. Many commentators applauded Ms. Huffman's guilty plea and her acceptance of the court's punishment for her deliberate and purposeful criminal act of mail and honest services fraud. Some followers of this ongoing case are hopeful that Ms. Huffman's guilty plea and obvious remorse for committing her crime will influence the other suspects in the case to accept responsibility for their fraudulent activity.

Justice will not be served until those who are unaffected are as outraged as those who are.

Benjamin Franklin (1706-1790)

Chapter 4

Fraud Detection Techniques

What are 'Fraud Risk Factors'?

Fraud risk factors relate to asset misappropriation and the adequacy of controls.

Adequacy of controls is the design, implementation and monitoring of the entity's control mechanism and its ability to detect and prevent fraudulent schemes and misappropriation of assets. If internal controls are weak such as lack of supervision, poor employee screening, weak accounting and physical controls, infrequent reconciliations, and lack of segregation of duties, then this can lead to the misappropriation of assets.

Misappropriation of assets is one of the most common frauds and can take different forms as follows:

- Cash theft is stealing cash from the company.

- Fraudulent disbursements are making fraudulent payments including payments to fictitious suppliers (fake billing schemes) or paying a fictitious employee (fake payroll schemes).

- Inventory Fraud is the theft of a company's inventory or stock.

- Misuse of Assets is the use of a company's assets by employees for their personal benefit.

The degree of susceptibility of fixed assets to theft also depends on the nature and type of assets. For example, assets with a high value, small in size, and in high demand are more likely to be misappropriated or stolen. The liquidity of the items is also important such as cash, jewels, and computer chips. There are countless examples of these robberies recorded in the press and indeed in history.

- In December 2004, thieves stole £26.5 million in cash from the Northern Bank headquarters in Belfast, Ireland. The authorities arrested five suspects, but they only recovered approximately £2 million in cash.

- The Antwerp Diamond Heist was the largest diamond heist in history. In February 2003, thieves escaped with more than $100 million worth of diamonds. In 2005, authorities arrested and convicted Leonardo Notarbartolo as the ringleader of the heist, but he never disclosed the identities of his partners in crime or the location of the stolen diamonds. The diamonds remain unrecovered.

- In January 2003, an organised gang stole £4.6 million worth of computer chips from London Heathrow airport. According to BBC news, Scotland Yard said the Pentium 4 chips were inside an unattended airlines' van. The thieves stole the van when the driver left it unattended.

What control mechanisms can we adopt to deter corruption?

We can categorise corruption into bribery, conflict of interest and extortion. Bribery is the most common type of corruption in organisations especially in vendor relationships and the bidding process for purchasing assets and/or awarding contracts. Internal controls concentrate on deterrence rather than detection as corruption is hard to detect.

Some of the controls a company can implement are:

- A well-documented and transparent policy for purchasing assets and awarding contracts. It is extremely important that one individual is not responsible for this job by frequently rotating trained employees and implementing segregation of duties.

- Most companies have strict policies on the value of gifts and benefits that vendors offer employees. In today's business world, companies often maintain a gift registry to ensure that any employee gift receipts from vendors are of nominal value. On the flip side, responsible vendors regularly inform client companies of bribery offers from company employees via hotlines numbers, advising senior management or calling the Human Resources department directly.

- As corrupt schemes often involve companies overpaying for goods and services, a good auditor will examine the cost of goods and services, analyse inventory and investigate inventory write-offs. They should also perform internal trend analysis to determine if procurement managers are purchasing unnecessary assets or paying above market value for essential assets.

What are the main benefits of using analytic procedures in an audit process?

There are three main types of analytical procedures:

1. Preliminary analytical procedures help the auditors plan their audit as it provides an insight into the company and helps to determine the high-risk areas.

2. Substantive analytical procedures are detailed evaluations of account balances by the auditors and the collation of evidence.

3. Final analytical procedures assess the company's final financial statements and the audit conclusions.

As well as the benefits mentioned above, the following are secondary benefits:

a. *Assessing the company's ability to remain as a going concern:* Evaluating the financial statements can help the auditors to determine if the company can continue to operate based on its current financial performance, market trends and the industry in general. A SWOT analysis is an additional tool used by many professionals today to measure the internal strengths and weaknesses of a company and to assess the external opportunities and threats in the market in which they operate.

b. *Indicating errors in the financial statements:* Analytical procedures can reveal if there is a variance between actual and expected results of the organisation which may be due to accounting errors and/or irregularities.

c. *Implications for detailed audit testing and procedures:* If the company results look reasonable, then the auditors can determine the level of audit testing required which would be considerably less than the testing required if the results appear inaccurate.

d. *Examination of the company's financial results using ratio trend analysis:* This examination can help to determine if the results of the company are in line with their industry peers.

What are the common rationalisations for a fraudster, which tempt him/her to commit acts of fraud?

We learned about the fraud triangle and the three items that need to be present in order to commit fraud. These are:

- Pressure and Incentive

- Opportunity

- Attitude and Rationalisation

Attitude and Rationalisation: Fraudsters often rationalise their behaviour and believe that they will repay the stolen money, or they have issues with top management and believe that they are entitled to steal from their employer.

- A person's moral values and their personal circumstances contribute to their inclination to commit fraud. They may be thieves and/or they are in financial hardship and need to steal to provide for themselves and their families (situation dependent criminal).

- They believe that they will avoid detection and the company management has no history of punishing or prosecuting people, meaning there is no deterrent.

- The company management and other employees are so corrupt that stealing is part and parcel of the company culture.

- Top management do not take risk management seriously or they do not communicate the importance of internal controls to middle management and employees.

- Internal controls are very weak.

- Forecasts and budgets are so unrealistic that employees inflate sales numbers for the relevant quarter or fiscal year to reach revenue targets to receive performance related bonuses.

- To achieve budget numbers, employees may not submit or record expenses related to the current accounting reporting period, so the company income appears higher than it is.

- Employees often take part in employee share purchase plans (ESPPs) and a public company's financial results impact the company's stock price so management and/ or employees may record fictitious revenue and/or lower expenses to influence the stock price for their economic benefit.

- Employee job dissatisfaction or frustration regarding losing out on a promotion that they believe they deserved which comes with a higher salary and extra benefits, so they think they are entitled to the extra money.

What important points should we consider when evaluating fraud risk factors?

According to SAS 99 which is Statement on Auditing Standards No. 99: Consideration of Fraud in a Financial Statement Audit, commonly abbreviated as SAS 99, the three main categories of fraud risk factors are management characteristics, industry characteristics, and operating characteristics (including financial stability). As such, evaluating the following factors is a cumulative process.

- *Management characteristics* are reflections of the management's ability, style and attitude, the company's internal controls, and the financial reporting process. It takes into consideration the management's motivation to carry out financial reporting fraud. Some tell-tale signs are increased involvement with and setting of accounting principles and practices for the company, setting unrealistic financial targets, promising increased dividend payments or stronger than anticipated stock performance to investors without any current financial information to back up these claims. Other warning signs are the quality of the board members and senior management, and the personnel turnover in both areas. The relationship between the management and the external auditor is especially important. There should be no strained relationships. These days, Chief Risk Officers (CROs) are increasingly popular in larger organisations and they work closely with the internal audit team and other members of the Executive Committee. Unfortunately, small organisations do not have the luxury of audit committees or even segregation of duties as there is normally just one accountant but company owners are normally heavily involved in the running and oversight of their businesses.

- *Industry characteristics* are the economic and regulatory aspects of the environment in which the business entity operates. The regulatory authority and its activities in the jurisdictions that the companies are headquartered is becoming increasingly important.

- *Operating characteristics* and financial stability include the nature of the business, the complexity of its financial transactions, where the company records financial transactions and disbursements, the geographic location of the company's operating activities, the company's profitability, and its general financial condition. Auditors spend a lot of time evaluating and testing the operating characteristics and financial stability of a company. Auditors must be diligent at every stage of their planned audit and will normally come across additional information at the following stages:

  1. Planning and risk assessment
  2. Discussions with management and staff

3. Audit tests such as control tests, substantive or analytical testing

4. Review of the audit

What circumstances may exist to create opportunities for management or other staff to commit fraud?

Again, we revisit the fraud triangle where three components must be present for fraud to exist.

- **Incentive and Pressure:** Sometimes managers and employees succumb to incentives or organisational pressures to commit fraud.

- **Opportunity:** This is not just the ability for the culprit to commit the fraud but also encompasses the belief that fraud can be committed without any penalties.

- **Rationalisation and Attitude:** Assuming that all other factors remain constant, a person's tendency to commit fraud is directly linked to their moral values and personal circumstances.

I believe the following circumstances may create opportunities for management or other staff members to commit fraud.

Weak or ineffective controls: Members of staff and senior management are usually involved in setting internal controls which is beneficial as this ensures that multiple viewpoints regarding risk factors are taken into consideration. However, this may also lead to employees identifying and exploiting loopholes during the task or upon completion of the process.

Company culture: If owners or management ignore theft and/or do not prosecute fraudsters, employees may think that it is okay to commit fraud as everyone else is doing it. In many cases, financial institutions like banks do not prosecute employees for stealing but compensate them to leave the company as negative press coverage could damage the company's reputation. Thieves often view this as a motivation to commit financial crimes.

Segregation of duties and supervision: If there is little segregation of duties and supervision including peer and management reviews, then this creates an opportunity for fraudsters to commit their crime. As the adage goes, "what gets measured gets done". If owners and management do not place enough emphasis on internal controls and do not inform the staff of the consequences of fraud, then the employees are unaware of how grave an offence that stealing is.

Company performance and/or excessive pressure on the organisation: If company results are not in line with executive management, board members or shareholders expectations then this often entices or forces employees to make questionable judgements regarding accounting entries, revenue recognition, and/or recording of expenses. We must remember that a lot of employees are dependent on bonus incentives, commissions, dividends, and stock performance. Every day we read about executive compensation and sometimes the bonus and stock option portions of their annual compensation which relies on the company's performance far exceeds their annual salaries.

The company's assets: As discussed earlier, the value demand and movability of a company's assets such as high demand and high value items, size, and convertibility to cash can tempt even an honest person to commit fraud. We must not forget the implementation of controls around protecting such assets, for example if we look at a jewellery store and all their high value assets, there needs to be strong physical security, supervision of employees, employee rotation to support segregation of duties, employee screening in the hiring process, accounting controls which includes correct inventory recording and frequent account reconciliations.

SAS 99 suggests that key sources for the identification of fraud risk factors are inquiries of Management. In this context, which type of questions should an auditor ask the management?

Management and others include executive management, internal audit team, audit committee and those inside the organisation who are directly involved with operational duties. I would be interested in knowing the following:

- What is the company's overall view on risk management, morals and business ethics? Have they communicated this to senior management and employees? How did they communicate this message to the employees – was it via email alerts, lunch and learns, internal online learning or other training programs? Is senior management in agreement with the organisation's opinion on risk management and fraud detection and prevention?

- Does management think that the financial statements of the company accurately represent the performance of the company? Has anyone requested management to alter or withhold information or make fictitious transactions or accounting entries?

- Are management aware or suspicious of fraud or fraudulent activities? Has anyone (internally or externally) reported fraud to them? What do they think are the high-risk areas for fraud in the organisation? What controls have they implemented to detect or prevent fraud?

- Are the internal controls well-documented and communicated to all levels within the organisation? Which department is responsible for maintaining and updating these controls? Does the company review these controls on an annual or a regular basis? Is internal audit involved in the control setting and annual review of these controls?

- Are reports prepared for executive management and the board of directors on the control environment annually or on a quarterly basis? This would include information on operating and divisional risk controls, including detection and prevention. It would also include information on the company's risk assessment procedures, communication and information systems and monitoring activities.

- I would expect external auditors to have open communication with the internal auditors. They should know what the internal auditor's opinion on fraud risk is, what reviews they have undertaken, what were their findings, did they identify any fraudulent activity or suspect fraudulent activity? What is their relationship with senior management like? What was the senior management reaction to actual or suspected fraudulent activity? Do they have access to all the information they need to do their job, or do they find it difficult to obtain information from management?

Case Study

Authorities charged and imprisoned a man for drug dealing. No drugs were ever found and the evidence against him was simply that he owned several properties but worked as a cleaner in a local factory. The implication was that the property purchases could only have been funded from the proceeds of crime. The man denied this. A forensic expert was instructed to review the man's financial affairs and explain how the man funded his lifestyle.

The expert made a detailed review of the man and his family's financial affairs, starting at the time he bought his first property. The records explained the sources of all the funds used to buy the properties. It showed how the man had used equity created through the legitimate purchase and sale of other properties to create his portfolio and support his family's lifestyle. The court accepted this fraud investigation report in its entirety and the man was released from remand without charge.

Based on the case study above, let us discuss the following:

What type of evidence do we think the expert would have gathered for his report?

Firstly, I would interview the suspect's employer, ask for a copy of all pay slips for the last twelve months and ask for information on the overtime and public holidays the man worked to determine his average annual income.

From the evidence obtained by the law enforcement, I would determine how many properties the man owned and obtain information from the suspect's legal representatives such as the property deeds for each of the properties to ensure they were legal purchases. In summary, most property deeds contain several essential elements to be legally operative.

- It must be in writing.

- The former owner (The Grantor) and the new owner (The Grantee) must have legal capacity to sign the documents.

- There should be an adequate description of the property.

- The operative word of conveyance must be present. All standard deeds include the necessary legal language that transfers the ownership of the property from one party to another.

- It must be signed by the grantor and legally delivered to the grantee (or someone acting on the grantee's behalf).

It would also be helpful to obtain the final sales and purchase agreement between the grantor and grantee to determine the amount paid for each property. I would also acquire the mortgage details on any and all of the suspect's properties.

If feasible, I would obtain a surveyor's appraisal of the properties. If this is not available, real estate agents are usually well-versed in the property values in certain areas or districts and normally volunteer opinions readily.

I would review any rental income if applicable.

All of this evidence would give me a better understanding of the income, expenses, and net worth of the individual in order to formulate an opinion.

Which documents could have helped the forensic expert in gathering evidence?

We must remember that even if the suspect did not generate his wealth from the drug dealing trade, they should be legal purchases and every taxpayer must pay any monies due to the Revenue Commissioners.

As well as the documents mentioned above as in property deeds, final sale and purchase agreements and the mortgage agreements, I would hope to gather the following documents and information:

- The suspect's bank statements to prove certain transactions, including the purchase and sale of the properties and rental income if applicable. Most banks issue hard copy or online statements to customers up to a period of twelve months and one can obtain additional statements for a small fee.

- Stamp duty records from the Revenue Commissioners, as in most countries stamp duty is payable on all properties.

I would expect the suspect's legal advisors to have records of these or I would approach the Revenue Commissioners directly. If no stamp duty was payable, then I would expect a record of this waiver.

- Capital gains tax declarations on all property sales. if no capital gains tax was payable then I would also expect a waiver to this effect.

- Rental income declaration on tax returns and recorded by the Revenue Commissioners.

If any of these documents hinted at any wrongdoings, then I would further investigate with the relevant authorities.

It is a fraud to borrow what we are unable to pay.
Publilius Syrus (fl. 85–43 BC)

Chapter 5

The Investigative Process

Explain the difference between proactive and reactive investigations?

We can divide financial crime investigations into two categories:

- Reactive

- Proactive

Reactive Investigations are the result of somebody (a whistle-blower) alerting the relevant authority to the fact that they think someone has committed a crime. The investigator will only react when an affected party has reported the crime. This is not only limited to company employees, management, internal and external auditors but a family relation can also inform the authorities of their suspicions. The suspect may be currently employed by the company or someone could report them after he/she has left.

I remember a story in the local newspaper when a bookkeeper of a shoe store noticed the cash receipts did not reach the store's bank account. The store manager processed all bank deposits. The bookkeeper informed the owner of the store who sent in forensic accountants and they collected enough evidence to prosecute the manager who admitted to stealing USD$100,000 in total. He was subsequently incarcerated. This is an example of a reactive investigation.

Proactive Investigations are a result of an investigator's findings. They do not wait for the aggrieved party to complain, but initiate action based on evidence of fraud.

A good example of this are financial regulators that monitor the activity of companies in its jurisdiction. Normally the regulator's employees are tasked with supervising a portfolio of publicly listed companies and observe the stock price of assigned companies daily. If there are unusual spikes or dips in the stock price, the supervisor takes into consideration any recent publicly available information or speaks with the company's assigned contact to ascertain the reasons behind the unusual activity. In other cases, the supervisor is aware of confidential and/or insider information pertaining to the company which may impact its share price fluctuations. The regulator makes an informed decision to investigate further or are satisfied with the company's explanations.

What is the difference between weighted and unweighted solvability factors?

Solvability factors refer to those characteristics of a case that indicate how successful the investigation is likely to be. Not all cases are solvable, so prioritising cases is essential. Identifying and discarding unsolvable cases leaves more time and resources for investigating those cases with a higher probability of solvability.

There are several solvability factors including the following:

- Witnesses to a crime and significant physical evidence retrieved at the crime scene.

- Knowledge of the suspect's identity and physical

description, home and employment addresses and any vehicle descriptions.

- Confidence that the crime may be solvable with a reasonable amount of additional investigative efforts.

We can classify solvability factors as weighted or un-weighted, but we must evaluate all cases on their merits regardless of the system used.

Weighted Solvability Factors: Weighted systems separate the more solvable factors from the less solvable ones. For example, physical evidence at the scene is more important than a witness to the crime.

Unweighted Solvability Factors: These systems do not assign weight to factors and all factors are equally important. These factors determine if the particular agency will investigate the case further or not. Casual observations rather than scientific analysis are the basis for unweighted solvability factors.

Why is goal setting and planning important for the soundness of the investigative process?

Complainants turn into an investigator's client(s). Criminal and civil cases produce different outcomes. Initially, the investigator should understand his clients' goals. Criminal cases usually involve fining and imprisoning the culprit. Civil cases are about repairing the damage to the victim, which typically takes the form of monetary compensation. The investigator must ensure his/ her clients are aware of possible outcomes and results to avoid encountering client dissatisfaction.

Obtainable result: This is the expected result based on the circumstances of the case and available technology. This not only applies to the current technology, but also future state technology as technological improvements usually emerge during the long lifespan of financial crime cases.

Acceptable outcome: This is the expected final outcome considering the current state of the law which is the constitutional limitation against backdated laws. For example, an acceptable outcome might be punishment that did not exist when the crime occurred but transpired during the lifespan of the case and is now enforceable.

Once the client is on board with the investigator's obtainable and acceptable outcomes of the investigation, they can set clear goals together. The investigator's progress and acceptability of the outcome are easier to evaluate objectively once both parties are on the same page.

Goals provide a solid foundation for the investigation to progress. An entire investigation is in jeopardy if goals are ill-defined, poorly designed or unrealistic. Developing a plan is the second task after defining the goals. The plan must be comprehensive and strong but requires flexibility to help manage some of the following aspects of a financial crime investigation:

- Information management. The amount of financial information can be overwhelming in a financial crime investigation, but a sound plan can help manage this feature of the investigation.

- Managing evidence. The volume of evidence is also an

aspect of the investigation that a sound plan will take into consideration. The plan also needs to consider the chain of evidence, which we discussed earlier.

- Accommodating changes. The plan must be flexible enough to incorporate new information and/or changes during the investigation.

What are the major objectives of an investigative plan?

There are three major factors involved in a sound investigative plan:

1. **Focus**: the investigative plan needs to align with the goals of the investigation, this means that no warnings signs and/or no leads are overlooked, and there is no duplication of tasks.

2. **Control**: the investigator needs to be in control of the case. Financial crime cases tend to get disorderly especially in relation to the amount of information under consideration. A well thought out and documented plan helps to manage investigations even when there is the inevitable influx of information and evidence.

3. **Adaptability**: we already determined that we need a strong plan, but financial investigations are constantly changing in terms of size and complexity. The plan must be able to take changes into consideration or the plan will be useless. Lack of flexibility will waste time on changing the plan, creating a new plan, or working with a temporary

plan which is never advisable. If something changes, then we would hope to tweak the plan rather than redrafting a new one.

What stages are involved in designing an investigative plan.

Firstly, there is pre-planning involved which is critical to avoid making quick, reactive, and ill-informed decisions. If investigators consider all possible scenarios, then they can contemplate all options when the need arises. They should consider and obtain all the support they need for the investigation ahead of time so they can prepare their plan. Planning does not prevent investigative hurdles; it simply makes them easier to manage and less detrimental to the outcomes. The following stages are critical to forming a strong and focused plan.

Financial Planning: There are always budget constraints to any project, and this is also the case for financial investigations. The clients want value for money and the investigator, by default, inherits the fiscal responsibility for the investigation. The client and investigator will usually have to compromise on financial decisions to minimise costs. Examples include phone tapping which appears relatively inexpensive until you consider the person-hours involved, as someone must listen to the recordings. An investigator may also need to supervise a surveillance team closely to avoid escalating costs. The investigator will need to consider alternative, less expensive investigative tools, or he/she might experience budget overruns which in turn can hamper the objectives of the investigation which leads to customer dissatisfaction.

Personnel Planning: After determining the scope and direction of the investigation, the investigator needs to have a personnel plan to hire the right people. The investigator will not have all the knowledge and skills for every facet of the case so he/she will normally engage external specialised consultants on a temporary basis. These experts are not only accounting and financial professionals, but also experienced technology consultants, as we are increasingly relying on today's digital age. The investigator needs to trust his/her external resources with a lot of sensitive data and may engage them at the planning stage of the investigation to form a solid and focused plan.

Technology Planning: In today's digital world, everything is computerised and investing in technology is necessary. Technology is expensive. The investigator must ensure that he has the right tools to do his/her job. An example of temporary investments is the renting of surveillance equipment while permanent investments include purchasing computer software and/or hardware. As technology is increasingly more important, the investigator will need to identify his/her technological needs in the planning stages and budget accordingly. Technology incompatibility is a major concern with computer software and hardware and the investigator will need to make wise purchases to ensure that his equipment is up-to-date and compatible with others. It is never possible to foresee all potential roadblocks with technology, but careful planning and forethought can help mitigate these risks.

What are the three primary areas in the intelligence gathering process?

The following three categories are a starting point for intelligence gathering, but the investigator might add more techniques and tools as the investigation progresses.

Surveillance: This is defined by Wikipedia as "the monitoring of behaviour, activities or other changing information of an individual". For the purposes of financial crime, investigators are interested in uncovering the following facts about the suspect or victim and the people close to them:

- Valuable assets they own such as boats, cars, fine jewellery, and expensive artwork.

- Real estate property and investment portfolios.

- The banks and financial institutions they patronise.

- Their key acquaintances the investigators can question and interview.

There may be no traceable documents in relation to the tangible assets they own but finding out about these facts early in the investigation can help investigators in the initial and latter stages of their enquiry.

Database Searches: Data is facts and statistics collected for reference or analysis, and databases are an organised collection of this data. Going one step forward, relational databases are structured together to recognise relations between stored items of information. Every transaction that takes place in the market economy is stored as data somewhere. These transactions include using debit and credit cards to access cash or purchase goods, renewing a driver's license or a passport and paid subscriptions to websites. It is imperative that investigators access relevant databases to analyse the information that will help them in their investigation. We can separate databases into two categories, which we will discuss later.

Trash Collection: We often hear about identity theft and criminals 'dumpster diving' in victims' trash bins for documents, such as credit card and loan applications or those containing social security numbers in order to use that person's information to fraudulently apply for credit cards and/or open bank accounts in the victim's name, et cetera. It is also a highly effective information gathering tool for investigators of financial crime, as people are careless about discarding receipts, documents and personal information. They may even discard evidence of their crime in the trash. There are trespassing laws regarding accessing an individual's property if the trash is on their property, but if the trash is on the street then it is not considered trespassing. This method of collecting information is often unpleasant and demeaning and most investigators avoid it if possible.

Databases

As I mentioned earlier, databases are organised collections of data and we can split them into two categories, public and private databases.

Private databases are databases with restricted access, and they may include government and commercial sources. Private databases can include sensitive data such as credit card information and private personal data. There are databases that the public can access for a fee, such as www.spglobal.com, which gathers, analyses and collates financial and investment data to provide insight into companies and their respective markets. Many people subscribe to this service and receive daily emails and real-time notifications on companies they monitor for general information and investment purposes.

Other databases store extremely sensitive information and are not available to the public. Law enforcement personnel and/ or government agencies can only access these for legitimate purposes. Unfortunately, these sites are subject to hacking, which has become increasingly common in the last decade.

Public data bases are generally available on the internet and available to the public free of charge. Examples of public databases are the U.S. Security and Exchange Commission at www.sec. gov, this website permits an individual to search for financial and other pertinent information on all publicly traded companies. I recently visited a government website and, although it was highly informative, it was difficult to navigate to the specific information I wanted which leads to the next point. The internet is full of information and combing through for specific information takes time and effort so when timeliness is critical, it is often speedier and cheaper to subscribe to private databases for a reasonable fee in an investigation.

Social websites such as Facebook and Instagram can be helpful in an investigation as people post personal pictures, videos, and information about their private life. There are common stories in the news where individuals break the law and boast about it on social media, members of the public alert the police and they, in turn, can easily identify and prosecute the culprit based on this evidence.

Why do financial crime investigations generally result in higher volumes of evidence and more complicated theories of evidence than non-financial crime?

Firstly, it is useful to list the stages of investigative plans for both financial and non-financial crimes:

- Initiation
- Planning
- Execution
- Prosecution
- Reflection

Earlier, we spoke about the initiation of financial crime investigations and the difference between reactive and proactive investigations. We also discussed the planning process. The next step is execution. This includes identifying witnesses, collecting documents, analysing, and assembling them into exhibits. When and if everything goes according to plan, the final step is charging a suspect. Financial crimes take longer, require more evidence and can be more complex than murder and non-financial crime investigations.

When we talk about complexity, we need to remember that there are so many fraudulent schemes which we learned about earlier –

from arson, credit card fraud, forgery and uttering to tax evasion and corporate fraud. The schemes may appear straight forward initially, but we often find out they are much more complicated once the investigation progresses as we are often dealing with intelligent, educated and calculating criminals. The business world is constantly changing and the introduction of new financial instruments, the increasing intricacy of company subsidiary structures, and international trade influences companies operating in business communities. Investigators need to collect vast amounts of financial records to support a conviction in complex financial crimes. Investigators spend a lot of time collecting background information on the company and the industry they operate in; this is also known as intelligence-gathering. We need to understand the company's organisational structure, operating processes and the controls they have in place. The investigator can also review public information concerning the company.

It is very important to know if the company is a cash business or uses accrual accounting. For example, a retail store is deemed a cash business, but an insurance company uses accrual-based accounting to determine both estimated premium income and claim expenses. The company employees and management should be able to provide the investigator with his/her information requests via documentation or interviews. Once the investigator absorbs and documents his/her understanding of this information then he/she relies on feedback from the company to confirm his/her understanding of their business.

The investigator should know the accounting standards applicable to the company based on their respective industry and the organisation that sets standards and general rules of practice or best practices. For example, The British Medical Association (BMA) is the trade union and professional body for doctors in the UK. These bodies provide a wealth of information regarding the industry and access to information via their websites or phone calls, which can be a valuable tool for the investigator to gather his/her information requirements. The investigator can also access information to non-professional organisations as they often publish information and literature about their clubs or societies, for example Rotary International.

All the information gathered in the investigation generates a lot of documentation and financial information which can be overwhelming, but it also gives the investigator confidence in his/her decision making. Based on the changing nature of investigations, regardless of the plan we spent so much time formulating, this reinforces the fact that the plan is more of an outline rather than a strict guidebook and needs to be flexible to incorporate changes.

Case Study

In 2015, Dave started a new job as manager of a public house in Yorkshire, England. He had years of experience in the pub trade but had never managed an entire pub before. He explained to the pub owner that he would need some help with book-keeping. The owner explained a system of record keeping and banking which he had devised himself. When the quarterly VAT return was due, the owner checked the records and found that there appeared to be a discrepancy in the banking. He complained to the police and they in turn charged Dave with theft of the shortfall and false accounting.

The defence instructed a forensic expert to review the accounting records and banking on its behalf.

The expert gave his opinion of the elements required in a properly designed accounting system for a pub and highlighted the many serious deficiencies in the system devised by the pub owner and the difficulties that Dave would have experienced in attempting to operate it. He also pointed to several probable causes of the cash discrepancy, other than theft by Dave. When the case came to court, the defence team presented several points in the report to the prosecution witnesses in cross-examination. At the close of the prosecution, based on the evidence, the judge agreed that Dave had no case to answer and then released him.

Consider the above case while we answer the following questions:

- What do we think could be lacking in the owner's self-devised accounting system? Firstly, the owner is a publican by trade so I would think he has limited knowledge and experience of accounting/bookkeeping systems. I am assuming that the system is computer based but I doubt that it is industry standard. If the owner devised the system then it may not be technologically sound, logic or intuitive to a third party like Dave.

- Did the accounting system have a bank reconciliation feature which compares the pub's bank statements to the transactions in the system and then produces reconciliation reports for a record of all reconciled transactions? This is a valuable tool as reconciling manually for a cash rich business like a pub can be labour intensive and prone to error.

- Did the owner have any external controls for recording cash in his record keeping system? For example, I worked for a retail business and I helped to create a daily spreadsheet for the owners to complete. They input the daily cash receipts, credit card receipts, customer credits and returns as per the cash register tapes. They then recorded the amount of physical cash from each register and the amount of credit card activity from the credit card machine reports. The spreadsheet calculated the difference between the cash register tapes and the amount of physical cash and credit card activity reports. The owner or the bookkeeper investigated any differences. The owners were pleased with this spreadsheet as it was relatively easy to populate, and the bookkeeper entered the amounts from these spreadsheets into the accounting system and reconciled to the bank statements on a monthly basis. This reasonably straightforward process also helped to raise the owners' awareness of their daily trade and strengthened their relationship with the bookkeeper.

- Another important feature of an accounting system is the financial reports feature. Does the accounting system have this feature? Weekly, monthly, quarterly and annual financial reports provide management and owners with valuable information about their business operations and flags discrepancies and inefficiencies which they can deal with faster.

Give some probable causes of shortfall other than theft by Dave.

An employee might be embezzling money from the pub. In Chapter 2, we spoke about the three factors we usually see in financial crime.

1. The presence of something valuable.

2. An opportunity to take something without being detected.

3. A perpetrator willing to commit an offence.

We also learned that given the opportunity, even the most truthful and trustworthy individuals may commit fraud and if the employee is under pressure then he/she may justify his/her actions. The cash is obviously something valuable and a change in management and lack of controls can give the culprit an opportunity. A pub is a cash business and is susceptible to embezzlement. I visited a pub recently and I was surprised by the number of cameras in the bar area, the manager informed me that in order to obtain insurance, they need cameras over every cash register and this simple investment in surveillance also served as a deterrent for employees to steal from the pub.

VAT returns include total sales and purchases. Bank statements record both sales and purchases. Purchases for the pub, amongst other items, would include purchasing alcohol and, in most cases today, food. Whilst the manager might oversee the purchases, a dishonest employee may be in collusion with the supplier and overpay the supplier so they can split the extra money.

If the owner, management or employees pay for purchases in cash from the till without adequately recording these transactions, then there is a high possibility that mistakes, or theft will occur.

There also may be counterfeit money in circulation and if the bank rejected the bank notes, it may not have been recorded in the accounting system. The pub might not have counterfeit detectors and/or may not be vigilant in inspecting large bank notes.

Corruption, embezzlement, fraud, these are all characteristics which exist everywhere.

Alan Greenspan
(American economist and former Chair of the Federal Reserve of the United States)

Chapter 6

Gathering Evidence

Note: Investigator can also refer to Forensic Accounting Investigator

What does the term 'best evidence' mean?

Best evidence does not refer to the most appropriate evidence to support a fraud accusation; it simply means that all evidence submitted should be original as secondary evidence, such as a copies or facsimiles, will not be admissible if the investigators can obtain original documents. Forensic investigators should always submit best evidence.

An example of this would be trying to prove that a senior company official stole money or defrauded the company using a sophisticated fraudulent scheme. Whilst copies of his/her bank statements would be acceptable evidence, unaltered original bank statements are best evidence. Forensic experts should collect all relevant evidence and as discussed in Chapter 5, we can then decide if we want to assign weighted or unweighted solvability factors.

Why it is important to keep the collected evidence in a well-organised manner?

Financial crimes differ from non-financial crimes as key evidence in a homicide, for example, would be physical evidence such as the murder weapon and fingerprints but most of the evidence for financial crime is documentation.

The amount of documentation in a financial crime can be overwhelming and investigators need to collect vast amounts of information to support a conviction especially in complex financial crimes. It is important to assemble evidence in a well thought out and orderly fashion to avoid 'getting buried' under all the paperwork accumulated throughout the investigation. We must try to avoid information overload, loss or destruction of documents and formulate a plan for storing documents before we start collecting data.

We need to consider the following:

Collection: We need to secure and package all evidence retrieved at the scene so there are no alterations to the documents and no damage during transportation. Storage boxes and envelopes will usually fulfil this need. Investigators cannot review and examine all documentation at the time of collection due to time restraints.

Storage: This refers to maintaining the integrity of the data to ensure it will be admissible in court. The investigators must store and use the evidence carefully. It is imperative there are no alterations to the original evidence and investigators should organise the evidence, so it is easy to identify and retrieve.

The Process of Proof: We can describe inference as the act or process of reaching a conclusion about something from known facts or concrete evidence. In court cases, it is the credible effect of each individual piece of evidence. Legally, conclusions drawn from inferences are proof.

Proof through Inference: Inference can be weak or strong depending on how easily a reasonable person can make a conclusion based on the evidence presented. Strong inference suggests that there is a close link between the evidence and the conclusion, while weak inference is the opposite. An example of weak inference is "the employee did not get along with management, so he stole the money" whereas a strong inference is "I saw the employee steal money from the petty cash lockbox". There are too many intervening steps between the weak inferences but the stronger second statement has fewer. The investigator's job is to minimise the steps between the evidence and the conclusion.

What devices can help us to collect evidence?

The following are examples of three devices often used to collect evidence.

Personal computers: The amount of evidence on work and private personal computers is enormous. People often forget IT departments monitor work computers, and all activities are traceable by user IDs which includes the recording of transactions in accounting and operating systems, emails, instant messages and access to any internet sites and/or searches. IT consultants can also access all information and history on work computers. Individuals who use private personal computers at home often access personal social media sites such as Facebook, Instagram and communicate regularly with family, friends and acquaintances via Skype and FaceTime and they seldom remember that there is a log of this activity. We regularly read about investigations in the news and social media where law enforcement agents capture and successfully prosecute suspects due to evidence they found on a criminal's personal computer, whether it is work issued or a private computer.

Personal Digital Assistants (PDAs) and Smart Phones: Like work and private personal computers, people are increasingly using these devices for sending emails, messaging and calling business and personal associates. Individuals often store contact details on these devices. In today's world, phone bills include details of all incoming and outgoing phone calls and text messages so there is a log of this activity which can be crucial in an investigation.

Security Systems: Security systems include but are not limited to the following: security guards, CCTV (closed-circuit television), cameras or other devices to monitor people entering and exiting buildings' doors, key-card access systems at buildings' entrances and exits. Each of these has its own merits. Security guards are physical witnesses. They can identify individuals and are often aware of dubious activity as they are highly trained in this area and/or are retired police officers. Most companies require a visitor to sign a guest book at the front desk detailing the person with whom they are meeting and times of entry and departure from the building. CCTV systems are useful in monitoring suspicious individuals and can be key evidence in all crimes not just financial ones. Key-card access systems records a log of company employee and/or consultants entering or exiting buildings. These systems are a useful tool when gathering evidence in suspected crimes as fraudulent employees often work late, at odd hours and/or over the weekend.

Which points should we consider when planning for the evidence gathering process?

As investigators, we should create a written plan concerning the collection of documents and data. This gives the investigation a clear direction and focus. It is important that we meet with the client(s) to discuss the type of evidence we may need and the location of the evidence relating to the period under scrutiny. In the planning stage, the following points are important for us to consider.

Technology: We require knowledge of the technology employed by the company to record transactions. For example, in an insurance company, the underwriters typically use a computer system to record customer policies. This can be a completely different system to the claims and accounting systems. Sometimes, these three systems are different modules in one database or there are interfaces between the separate systems. We need a solid understanding of how the company's technology works.

IT back-up: We need to know about the company data back-up policy for IT systems within the organisation. These policies normally apply to all equipment and data owned by the organisation and data back-ups usually occur at the end of every working day. It is important to know if the company complies with these policies. We also need to know if the company archives these back-ups off-site and information about the ability to restore this data; the client should be able to provide us with this information.

Records: There are many opinions about how long a company should retain business records, known as its document retention policy. There are different government bodies and regulators that often dictate the length of time that records are kept. As a rule of thumb, companies retain tax returns, supporting documents, business ledgers and other key records for seven years. Business asset records are usually held indefinitely. If these assets are sold, then the records are normally kept up to a year after the sale. Human Resources should keep employees' records from three to ten years depending on the circumstances, which can include the employee's length of service and if there were any legal issues during the employee's tenure and/or termination with the company. Due to limited filing space, companies often archive documents off-site with an external document management company and as investigators we should have access to these facilities.

Information: Any information held by current or former employees on their personal computers. Companies can discover if employees obtain company information by examining emails sent to personal email accounts especially those including attachments. Work computers also detect removable devices that employees use to download (or steal) company data and this information is frequently stored on company servers. Inspecting employees' home computers can also reveal any company information that should not be in their possession.

Company Hierarchy: We should also familiarise ourselves with a company's organisational hierarchy, which depicts the organisational structure and who reports to whom. It is important to have diagrams depicting the entire organisation and illustrating the relationship between employees. Many companies have these readily available, as company boards, senior management, rating agencies, and investors request these on a regular basis.

What type of information do 'working papers' contain?

Sometimes, it is necessary for the investigator to testify in court about certain facts obtained during his/her investigation or the law may require him/her to produce these in front of regulatory bodies. He/she will rely on working papers compiled during the investigation, which summarises and analyses factual material including supporting documents. All investigations differ from one another but working papers often include the following documents:

Accounting records and other documents: These include but are not limited to the following – accounting records such as general ledgers and journal entries, public and internal management financial reports, internal and external audit reports, bank statements and reconciliations, vendor and customer information, contract agreements, fixed asset records, and computer and security system records.

Public record searches: Investigators can conduct simple internet searches, newspaper articles and social media presence about the individual(s) or company under investigation. As mentioned earlier, investigators have access to public information filed by regulated entities and can easily retrieve this information from public websites.

Electronic computer files: These include emails, information from company issued or private devices and files on company or home computers.

Photographs or digital photos: Preferably with a date/time stamp.

Documentation specifying a chain of custody.

Interview notes and audio recordings: These include notes and recordings of statements from victims, suspects and third parties.

Third-party information: This is information from interested or connected third parties such as legal counsel, auditors, and financial institutions. This can include banking documentation, audit reports, documents obtained through warrants or subpoenas, and any other relevant documents or evidence.

Court pleadings and deposition transcripts: Pleadings are formal written legal statements that parties file in a lawsuit to communicate their complaints or defences to a claim in a civil action. A deposition transcript is a recording of evidence given under oath in a court of law.

What are the main steps involved in the evidence gathering process?

Forensic accounting investigations focus on gathering, documenting and retaining evidence. The conclusions drawn from investigations depend on the credibility of the evidence. Therefore, it is important that we gather, preserve and store evidence in a proper manner. We can expect to gather a lot of evidence over the course of an investigation and it is important to know what to keep. Sometimes, it is wise to keep all evidence as a court ordered writ, such as a subpoena may require the investigator to present all evidence.

The following are critical steps in gathering evidence:

1. Planning Consideration

A plan not only indicates the scope of the investigation, but also helps to map out the relevant documents required by the investigator(s). It also helps the investigators to avoid accumulating excessive amounts of information and helps them to centralise the storage of evidence. This is often the preferred method as opposed to storing in multiple locations.

Planning can help the forensic accountants to focus on the information they require as culprits often try to confuse them with terminology and company jargon. Knowing the exact names of the company's management and statutory reports is the best way to avoid part of this problem. Internal and/or external auditors can provide this information.

2. Document Retention Gathering

Due to the nature of financial crime, investigators rely on documentary proof. They place high importance on document retention and preservation. It is wise for investigators to work with legal counsel to discuss some basic points regarding document and evidence preservation. For example, which documents and evidence they should obtain and for what length of time. Investigators also need to safeguard electronic data obtained from accounting and other operational systems. They can save the data they require via a data dump, which is downloading the data from the company systems to a disc or USB flash drives. This will give them the data at the beginning of the investigation and as it is static data, it safeguards the data from manipulation or destruction as the investigation progresses.

3. Creating a Chain of Custody

The investigator should discuss the level of detailed record-keeping with the client and legal counsel before gathering evidence. The evidence should be sufficiently useful to prove something important in a trial.

As discussed in earlier chapters, an investigator needs to follow the chain of custody when gathering evidence which is the movement and location of physical evidence from the time the investigator obtains the evidence until the time he/she presents it in court and a well-organised assembly of evidence is a must to achieve this objective.

What types of documents should we collect in the evidence gathering process and what could be the possible sources for these?

The type of documents includes the following:

Signed Statements: These include written and signed statements from the complainant and witnesses. Whilst they may not be admissible in court, the investigator is aware of the circumstances of the case and the testimony they may provide during the trial.

We often read about individuals changing their stories over time, so it is important to obtain written and signed statements at the beginning of the investigation.

Transactional paperwork: While all companies operate differently, most businesses generate the same paperwork with regards to bank statements, invoices, payments and accounting or bookkeeping records, regardless of whether it is in a manual or computerised format.

Intranet Sources: More companies are using intranets which are internal websites for company employees. These websites supply a wealth of information including organisational structure, colleague information and contact details, departmental and company policies, regulatory filings, share price information, noticeboards and internal chatrooms or instant messages. Company employees often forget that work computers are company property and all transactions and communication history is stored on servers. Employees can get careless and reveal too much information in instant message exchanges and chatroom discussions.

Emails: Large volumes of emails are exchanged daily and these are often stored on company servers. People use company email systems for business and personal purposes and can send emails to the wrong person or include sensitive and/or confidential information in error. The investigators can search for email evidence and as some people do not use email but prefer internal memos, investigators can also review these in their quest to find out if the suspect is guilty.

Regarding the sources of documents, the investigators should gather evidence from the following and best practice suggests that we should follow the order below:

The Victim of Financial Crime: Regardless of the fact, if the victim is an individual or a group of individuals who were defrauded or a company who lost millions of dollars to financial crime, these are the first port of call when collecting evidence. For example, individual victims can show bank and investment statements or any other evidence that alerted them to the fraud. Companies can also provide documented evidence and internal or external audit findings. It is important for investigators to collect and keep this evidence, so it is not subject to damage. Sometimes, the victim is unwilling to give original information to the investigators so they should present a copy, and in turn, the investigator will issue a receipt for said documentation.

Third parties who may have access or possess documentary evidence. Most of the documentary evidence collected in a financial crime is from third parties. A criminal is like any other individual and will have contact and communication with other businesses, financial institutions and seek advice from third parties. He/she also needs access to these third parties to commit the financial crime.

Generally, we can break down the suspect's contacts into five categories:

1. Financial Sector: including banks, insurance professionals, and brokerage houses.

2. Professionals: such as lawyers, accountants, and investment advisors.

3. Industry Contacts: such as business organisations, network groups, and associations.

4. Government.

5. Personal Contacts: These may or may not be involved in the fraud but nevertheless have vital information about the suspect.

Evidence possessed by the suspect: Investigators often approach the suspect for documented evidence at the end of their document collection. The investigators should familiarise themselves with the suspect's behavioural patterns about his personal and business activities to gain knowledge of the suspect and to avoid making faulty judgements and/or missing or discarding important evidence. Collecting evidence from the suspect may be difficult and may depend on if it is a criminal or civil case. We should always remember that the consensual production of documents by the suspect is a strong tool and we must not underrate it.

What types of evidence are used in financial crime investigations?

The Chambers dictionary defines evidence as *"information, et cetera that gives grounds for belief; which points to, reveals or suggests something"*, it also describes it as *"written or spoken testimony used in a court of law"*. All relevant evidence should be admissible in court as it serves to prove a fact. Evidence results in the emergence of proof. The burden of proof is a party's responsibility to prove or disprove a fact. In criminal cases, the burden of proof is the obligation of the prosecutor as suspects are innocent until proven guilty.

There are several types of evidence:

Direct Evidence is evidence that proves a fact without making any presumptions or inference for example if a witness saw the defendant steal money then this is direct evidence. In direct evidence, the witness re-counts what he/she experienced.

Circumstantial Evidence is described as evidence drawn from a conclusion or verdict but not proven. Circumstantial evidence is also known as indirect evidence. Circumstantial evidence needs to prove several supporting facts, analyse them in relation to others to prove that the ultimate fact in question exists. For example, if a witness saw the defendant steal money then this is direct evidence, whereas if the witness saw the defendant enter an office vault, heard commotion and then saw the defendant exit the building with a stuffed gym bag, this is circumstantial evidence as the witness did not physically see the theft.

Oral Evidence is spoken testimony given by witnesses in court, usually under oath. It includes witness accounts and presentations during submission of records and physical objects. It provides additional knowledge and insight about topics in question before the court.

Documentary Evidence includes written material and any other official or private writing introduced in a trial such as official documents, deeds, memos, private diaries entries et cetera. In addition to written evidence, it also includes other media such as photographs, videos, printed emails and tape recordings.

Real or Physical Evidence consists of tangible objects or property. Some professionals call this evidence material evidence. It must be relevant to the case and admissible in a court of law.

Evidence should be relevant, significant to the outcome of a trial and admissible in court. Hearsay which is third-hand information, rumour or gossip is not admissible in court. Confessions are formal statements by culprits admitting that they committed a crime, are facts and are not hearsay. Usually, written admissions or oral statements are evidence and can also serve as information to discredit a witness.

What are the basic differences between evidence gathered in financial crime cases versus non-financial crime cases?

Evidence collected during any crime is vital for the investigation. It is an effort and time-consuming task, especially in financial crime investigations. Two differences between financial and non-financial crime evidence are:

Physical evidence in financial crimes involves collecting a lot of documentary evidence such as financial statements, bank statements, invoices, receipts and other physical and/or electronic documentation which leads to a lot of paperwork.

Physical evidence at non-financial crime scenes, such as a homicide, include murder weapons, blood samples, fingerprints, footprints, and any other property left by the perpetrator, such as a wristwatch.

Credibility of witnesses and their testimonials: witnesses to a financial crime usually consist of educated white-collar workers and they are more likely to collaborate with law enforcement. These witnesses can also be the individuals who instigate the investigation by alerting the relevant departments or authorities via hotlines. According to the 2018 RTTN, organisations with hotlines detect fraud by tips more often than those companies with no hotlines. In actual fact, the 2018 RTTN reports that employees provide over half of tips and nearly one-third of tips come from outside parties.

Sometimes, witnesses to non-financial crime can be involved in the committed felony under investigation. The witnesses can be different individuals from any social class and authorities must deal with a wide range of personality and motivation factors. Witnesses to a non-financial crime may have a criminal history and their incentive to cooperate with authorities might be problematic.

I believe in evidence. I believe in observation, measurement, and reasoning, confirmed by independent observers. I'll believe anything, no matter how wild and ridiculous, if there is evidence for it. The wilder and more ridiculous something is, however, the firmer and more solid the evidence will have to be.

Isaac Asimov (1920-1992)

Chapter 7

Obtaining and Evaluating Non-Financial Evidence

The following are examples of non-financial sources of evidence:

- Body and eye language
- Statement analysis and SCAN
- Handwriting analysis
- Interviews

Body and Eye Language

There are some sure giveaway signs for fraud examiners to watch for when they are interviewing a possible perpetrator. A person displays his/her emotions by their facial expressions and gestures. A person's speech tends to speed up and they adopt a higher pitch of voice when they are lying. Crossed arms can indicate anxiety and a lack of trust, crossed legs indicate a negative attitude. All of these could indicate deception. Unfortunately, even body language experts can get it wrong as human beings' actions and reactions differ in certain situations. Due to this and the circumstantial nature of reading body language as a deception-detecting tool, it is not admissible in court as evidence.

Visual Access Cues (VAC) refers to the language of the eyes and the principles related to it. Some regard it as a more reliable indicator of truthfulness. It involves the eyes moving up and to the left or right for visualisation. Blinking is also part of eye language principles and when a person is under stress, he/she tends to blink quite rapidly (this also happens if they lack sleep or are on TV, so we need to take this into consideration). If a person gazes downwards, this can indicate guilt or defeat, raised eyebrows indicates surprise, disbelief or frustration and someone who raises one eyebrow with a tilted head is displaying arrogance or contempt. Eye language when combined with good interviewing techniques can lead to reliable interpretations and results.

Statement Analysis and SCAN

According to research, at least 90% of statements made are truthful, and most people do not attempt to lie directly. Statement analysis examines a statement word by word and assesses the truthfulness of the statements. The examiners analyse the words used rather than focusing on the truthfulness of the stated facts. Advocates claim they can use this technique to detect concealed information, missing information, and whether the information provided by the person is true or false. An example of this is deceitful people often start out with statements such as 'I' did this and later 'I' changes to 'we', they may also use a possessive pronoun such as 'my files' and later refer to it as 'the files' in order to distance themselves from the crime. Due to the observational nature of statement analysis, it is generally not admissible in court.

SCAN which stands for Scientific Content Analysis, tries to detect deception rather than obtain truthfulness and is similar to statement analysis. Fraudsters tend to deceive indirectly rather than tell obvious lies. The indirect deception involves leaving out critical facts, pretending to be forgetful or feigning ignorance and using words that dissociate them from the event. SCAN studies speech patterns, seeking tell-tale signs of deception by analysing both structure and contents of statements. Some say SCAN is as effective as a polygraph and like a polygraph, it is inadmissible in court.

Handwriting Analysis

Graphology is the analysis of the physical characteristics and patterns of handwriting that seeks to identify the writer, evaluate personality characteristics and assess the psychological state of the individual at the time of said writing. Handwriting analysis has been controversial for many decades and some courts of law place little reliance on it.

Interviews

Interviews are structured conversations. During forensic investigation interviews, it is important to ask the right questions and to ask them in the correct way. The interviewer should be familiar with the legal protocol of interviews and have experience and knowledge of specific interviews. We do not want the interviewer to botch the interview and/or receive a countersuit from the suspect.

There are certain questions asked during interviews:

1. Introductory
2. Informational
3. Assessment
4. Closing
5. Admission-seeking

The interviewer should prepare well thought-out open-ended questions and have good social skills to develop a relaxed rapport with the interviewee. The interviewer should also listen more so the interviewee can speak more. The interviewer should also note the body language of the suspect and take his/her time when asking questions. They should ask follow-up questions if necessary, as honest people do not mind elaborating whereas a fraudster tends to become agitated and annoyed. Once the interviewer has obtained all the facts, he or she should also confirm the facts he/she has obtained during the interview.

What is the difference between asking questions in an audit and those asked in a fraud investigation?

Internal and external auditors will ask questions during their audit. They usually ask these questions verbally, via email, telephone calls and even in instant messages. This is not the case in a fraud investigation. In a fraud investigation, the investigator will ask the questions in an interview setting which they may visually or audibly record. An interviewer should use best practice and prepare open-ended questions rather than those requiring yes or no answers.

The interviewer ought to dress appropriately, have a relaxed demeanour, be polite and relate well with the interviewee. They should ask well-placed questions, not too fast, not too slow or too long so the interviewee is comfortable with the process. The interviewer should avoid writing out the questions. The questions should be easy to understand and flow easily. In a regular audit, auditors are usually communicating with qualified accountants so they ask more technical questions – this should not be the case in a fraud investigation, as we do not want to intimidate the interviewee. As discussed earlier, the interviewer should listen more than speak, they should ask follow-up questions for clarification and recheck the facts they learned during the interview. A good interviewer will also observe any deceptive body language and gestures displayed by the interviewee.

The main objective of an interview with a suspect in a fraud investigation is for the suspect to become the subject of the interview and to obtain a signed confession from him/her – this is an admission-seeking interview. This differs from an audit, as auditors usually meet with company employees to gain further understanding about a process or to gather back-up documentation and working papers for specific transactions they are examining.

What interviewing techniques should we consider when we speak with a financially sophisticated suspect and/or witness?

We learned in previous chapters that there is a correlation between a culprit's seniority in the company and the severity of the loss. For example, in the United States, the median amount stolen by owners or executives is USD$637,000. People with good educational backgrounds and higher levels of intelligence commit bigger and more sophisticated fraud schemes.

Financial fraud schemes are usually very intricate and complex, and the interviewers should prepare by trying to understand the workings of these complicated schemes. Financially sophisticated suspects and witnesses tend to be arrogant and often try to confuse authorities with industry terminology and jargon.

The interviewer should have well prepared questions. They should be confident and avoid the suspect/witness feeling intimidated. The interviewer needs excellent interpersonal skills and should lead the interview rather than allowing the suspect/witness to take control of the interview and digress from the questions. The interviewer should also remain measured and calm throughout the interview. The interviewer will probably ask a lot of follow-up questions in the interview for his/her understanding and clarification. The investigators may even need to hold additional interviews with the suspect/witness.

We will be covering more interviewing techniques in Chapter 8.

All men are frauds. The only difference between them is that some admit it. I myself deny it.

H.L. Mencken (1880-1956)

Chapter 8

Interviewing Techniques

How does interviewing help the financial crime investigators in their work?

As discussed, interviews are purposeful conversations, crime investigators may interview several people including the victim, the suspect, and witnesses to a crime. This can be a simple question and answer style interview or a complex in-depth conversation.

An interview is a fact-finding mission and asking the right questions should lead investigators to the truth. Careful interview planning is a crucial step undertaken by the investigative team.

The main objective of an interview with a suspect in a fraud investigation is for the suspect to become the subject of the interview and to obtain a signed confession from him/her. This is also known as an admission-seeking interview.

What is the first stage in planning the interview?

The investigators need to establish whom they will interview. Due to the very nature of the crime, there are relatively fewer witnesses in a financial crime when compared to a regular crime. Financial crime is usually committed in secrecy and involves crafty planning. Most financial crimes often mirror a legitimate business transaction. To successfully execute the crime, the perpetrator relies on the absence of eyewitnesses. We learned in earlier chapters that financial crime investigations are usually reactive investigations, which means that citizens/victims initiate the investigation by complaining to the relevant authorities (also called whistle-blowers). The investigator will only react when an affected party reports the crime, for example, an employee, spouse, customer, shareholder, member of management or an auditor.

The investigator can have a number of other potential witnesses other than the whistle-blower, including accountants, auditors, banking personnel and business consultants who may have dealings with the suspect. We cannot dismiss them as they may have important information about the suspect which we cannot overlook.

We should always interview current and previous employees. Previous employees usually have no current relationship with their former bosses so they may be willing to speak more candidly about what they witnessed or suspected during their employment whereas current employees may be loyal to their employers and might be less forthcoming with information. The investigator needs to keep in mind that witnesses may resent the suspect and distort facts, lie and/or concoct fake stories. It is therefore incredibly important to double-check negative statements.

We normally interview the actual suspects of the case towards the end of the interview process. However, if the suspect is at risk of destroying evidence, leaving their place of employment or issuing threats to witnesses, then we should interview the suspects earlier in the investigation. Studies have found that one of the simplest questions to ask a suspect is "Did you do it?". The reason being some perpetrators want to confess and sometimes you just need to ask this question.

Which type of interviewees could we consider when investigating financial crimes?

In addition to the witnesses we identified above, we also mention possible contacts in Chapter 6, and we broke these down into five categories:

1. **The Financial Sector:** Banks, insurance professionals and brokerage houses. Investigators may gain access to critical information through paper trails left by the suspect's interaction with his/her bank and valuable information from interviews with the suspect's bank manager. This also applies to investment and pension advisors.

2. **Professional contacts:** such as lawyers and accountants. Lawyers may have information regarding property and other valuable assets and corporate meeting minutes and documents. The accounting firm may have working papers pertaining to sources of income, expenses, loans and hidden accounts as well as tax returns information. Due to their professional ethics, lawyers and accountants typically work with authorities.

3. **Suspects:** They often interact with business organisations, networking groups and associations within his/ her respective industry. The investigators can review information regarding the industry and can use data provided by these organisations as a baseline to compare

the earnings and business activities of the suspect with his/her peers.

4. **Government records:** In an increasingly regulated business environment, investigators can find out an enormous amount of information about the suspect and his/her business dealings from government records. Property, legal and personal records are often available to investigators and authorities at little or no cost.

5. **Personal Contacts:** Lastly, the financial criminal will have personal contacts that may not be involved in illegal activities but may possess essential information. Personal contacts include spouses, partners, exes, family members, et cetera. They will also know the suspect's character, personality traits and moral values, as well as their additional valuable possessions which may be concealed from authorities and the general public.

Why is it important to record the interview?

It is important for us to record the interview, preferably a videotaping over an audio recording, so we can perform statement analysis and study the suspect/witnesses body language after the interview. We do not want to intimidate the suspect and/or witnesses, so we usually limit the number of interviewers present in the meeting to a maximum of two persons. As the interviewers are busy carrying out the actual interview and due to the very nature of conversations, they can miss valuable information offered by the suspect and/or witnesses during interviews, so reviewing the recording at a later date is valuable. Other investigative personnel may want to review the interviews as they may have more experience or additional skills which may help with the investigation. A recorded interview is also evidence that is usually admissible in court.

What is the importance of where we conduct the interview?

The locations of the interviews are important. The investigators should schedule meetings which are convenient to the witness, the organisation and the investigators themselves. They should hold them during normal business hours and at times where the suspect and/or witness has a lighter than normal workload. Investigators prefer in-person interviews as telephone interviews are poor substitutes and a videoconference is only marginally better.

The interviewer should interview the suspect/witness in a location where they feel comfortable such as his/her office, home or even a neutral place, such as a hotel lobby. Investigators should refrain from conducting interviews in a bar, parking lot or private vehicle and the interviewers should be mindful of their own personal safety, which is why interviews in government buildings are more secure and they usually have screening devices to detect weapons.

Some witnesses want to conduct interviews on their own turf, but this might hinder the success of the interview or obtaining a confession as the interviewee will feel less pressure in his/her familiar environment. There are pros and cons to every location and there is a fine balance between conducting an interview where the interviewee will feel more at ease, which can lead to an open, honest and frank conversation and where the investigator will have the psychological upper hand in his/her work environment.

What stages are involved in the interview planning procedure?

Who?

As we discussed earlier, there are relatively fewer witnesses to financial crime, the crime is usually committed covertly, and the crime can look like a regular business transaction. Therefore, it is important not just to interview the witnesses but previous employees, business associates, personal friends and acquaintances.

What?

After identifying the interviewees, as investigators we need to plan what to discuss with them. People can rarely give eyewitness accounts due to the secretive nature of the crime. In Chapter 3, we also spoke about the diverse types of criminals, when we studied power brokers. They are usually very competent employees and have detailed knowledge of accounting systems, including the system's weaknesses and loopholes. We should also remember that business associates are more removed from the crime, and as such, in the case of the suspect's bank manager, they may be able to provide vital information such as where the fraudster hid the money as financial crimes are all about 'following the money'. In recent years, financial institutions are increasingly concerned about money laundering and its compliance with financial crime legislation. Therefore, bank officials and managers have a duty to disclose relevant information to investigators. They may also have documentary evidence that is critical to the case which they can share with investigators.

Why?

An investigator should be able to easily explain why he needs to interview a witness based on who they are and what information they may have relevant to the case. We also discussed the importance of determining the timing and order of the interviews. Investigators usually interview accountants and bankers as they normally have background information in the information gathering stage, and accounting clerks with more detailed information at a later stage. Both kinds of information are of equal value, but we should obtain them at various stages.

When?

The investigators should try to schedule meetings at times and days of the week that are convenient to the interviewees. As we mentioned earlier, this should be when their workload is lighter than normal. It is also better to allow the interviewee to determine the time of the meeting rather than the investigators dictating the time. We must remember it is important to create a relaxed and friendly atmosphere for the witness, so we have his/her full cooperation.

Where?

We addressed the importance of conducting an interview in a location where the interviewee will feel at ease, which can lead to an open, honest and frank conversation, and where the investigator will have the psychological upper hand in his/her work environment.

Investigators should hold interviews in a private office or designated interview room. The room should be free of distractions such as telephones or two-way radios as they can cause unexpected distractions. All participants should turn off cell phones and pagers. The room should be as basic as possible – a desk and enough chairs for the interview participants. There should be no potential weapons such as letter openers, scissors or staplers within the subject's reach.

The interviewer should place a 'Do Not Disturb' sign on the door. The interviewer should make every effort to minimize the number of reminders of punishment in the room. If possible, the subject should not be able to see signs of law enforcement presence such as handcuffs or an 'Investigator of The Year' plaque. Investigators should take care to ensure that the interviewees have access to an exit that is not blocked by the interviewers. This is a safety consideration, but also may be a consideration to demonstrate the voluntary nature of statements.

How?

The investigator has many options in terms of how to interview the witness. The tone of the interview is especially important. The interviewers can develop rapport by displaying objectivity, fairness and professionalism at all time. They should also introduce themselves and ask the interviewee who they are and what they do. To create a comfortable interview setting, the interviewer should show respect and courtesy to the interviewee and should be non-threatening in their demeanour.

We should plan to have a videotape, audiotape or a handwritten recording of the interview. There are a few reasons to record interviews:

- It protects the interviewer: The interviewee cannot accuse the interviewer of making any statements they did not make, and we can quickly dismiss any false accusations of the interviewer making threats.

- Recordings also protect the interviewee: When there is an actual recording of what he/she said, no one can restate his/her words inaccurately.

- We already spoke about the importance of videotaping over audio recorded so we can study the suspect/witnesses body language after the interview. To have a better idea of what happened in the interview, it is preferable to have images to accompany sounds such as loud banging which may be attributable to a palm slamming a table or an object falling in the interview room.

- Even though there is a risk that someone will destroy or steal recordings, they last longer than the average person's memory. In case of a number of witnesses or complex topics discussed, recordings can be a godsend.

- Interview tapes assist with trial preparation and they help to prevent investigators forgetting vital details and amending statements incorrectly.

We must be mindful that whilst interviews can be remarkably effective, there is also a possibility of errors in remembering events.

A technique that recalls a lot of information also increases the possibility of error in recollection. Supporting evidence, especially documentary evidence, in financial crime can support the evidence obtained by investigators in interviews.

If you see fraud and do not say fraud, you are a fraud.
Nassim Nicholas Taleb (Essayist, scholar and statistician)

Chapter 9

Fraud Risk Assessment

What factors do we need to consider for a fraud risk assessment?

The probability of an event occurring, and the impact of that event forms the foundation of a risk assessment. We can calculate the level of risk as the product of the probability that harm occurs (e.g. that an accident happens) multiplied by the severity of that harm (the average amount of harm or more conservatively the maximum credible amount of harm).

We consider a range of factors for a risk assessment. Initially, we usually consider factors at the entity level, such as organisation size, fraud types, the industry the company operates in and the divisions within the company.

According to the 2018 RTTN, the total loss caused by the cases in its study exceeded $7 billion with an average loss per case of $130,000. Asset misappropriation occurred in more than 89% of cases and caused a median loss of $114,000 whilst financial statement fraud occurred in less than 10% of cases but caused a median loss of $800,000.

The 2018 RTTN also looked at the size of the organisations and the frequency of fraud. Small organisations (with 100 employees or less) were the most common victims of fraud with 28% of cases whilst larger organisations (with 100-999 employees or more) accounted for the fewest cases at 22%.

The top three victim industries with reported cases of fraud were:

1. Banking and financial services reported 366 cases and incurred a median loss of $110,000.

2. The manufacturing industry reported 212 cases and experienced a median loss of $240,000.

3. Government and public administration reported 201 cases and suffered a median loss of $125,000.

The median loss by industry was surprisingly different to the number of cases reported by industry:

Industry	No. of cases	% of Cases	Median Loss
Communication & Publishing	24	1.1%	$525,000
Energy	94	4.4%	$300,000
Professional Services	58	2.7%	$258,000

The 2018 RTTN looked at the frequency of fraud schemes and median losses within different departments. Fraud was especially high in accounting departments with 14% of cases causing an average loss of $212,000. The next biggest offender was operations departments with 14% of cases causing an average loss of $88,000. Executive/upper management were responsible for 11% of cases but the median loss was a staggering $729,000.

The 2018 RTTN also examined the frequency of fraud schemes and the different sub-schemes. Asset Misappropriation accounted for at least 89% of cases and losses incurred in cheque and payment tampering (12% of cases) causing an average loss of $150,000. Billing schemes rated as significant (20% of cases) with an average loss of $100,000, a billing scheme is a fraud directed at the payment system of a business and can result in the company making a fraudulent payment to an employee but appears as a valid business expense. The 2018 RTTN also found the most common reason for asset misappropriation schemes than other forms of fraud was due to lack of management review.

What are the main concepts of a risk assessment?

A fraud risk assessment depends on the investigator's knowledge of fraud concepts, which includes the following:

1. The Fraud Triangle
2. Fraud Indicators
3. Fraud Schemes

Accounting information systems and an understanding of the fraud environment, which includes timeframe, entity, effectiveness of internal controls, et cetera.

We discussed the fraud triangle several times in earlier chapters, the fraud triangle consists of the following:

1. **Motive** or pressure to commit fraud, for example, the perpetrator has a financial difficulty he/she needs to solve.

2. An **opportunity** to commit the fraud, the person must see some way that he/she can solve his/her financial difficulty with a low perceived risk of discovery.

3. **Rationalisation** – the thief can justify his/her reason for the fraud to him/herself and others for example, he/she says they were just borrowing the money and were fully intending on paying it back.

Fraud Indicators are found during audits and/or examination of financial statements and generally include but are not limited to unusual sales patterns, unusual financial ratios, irregularities in documentation, recognition of revenue that is not consistent with contractual terms, long-outstanding debts, non-reconciled accounting entries, irregularities in inventory, large credit notes after year-end, et cetera.

There are many fraud schemes ranging from credit card fraud, arson, loan sharking, bribery, skimming, embezzlement, stock fraud and manipulation, tax evasion, bank fraud, government contract fraud as well as extortion, mail order procedures, financial statement schemes and identity theft amongst many others. Some of these schemes are extraordinarily complex and difficult to understand.

It is also useful if the investigator has adequate knowledge of accounting information systems and understands the fraud environment which includes timeframe, entity, and effectiveness of internal controls. Many accounting systems have accounts payable, accounts receivable and a general ledger module. The investigator should understand the basic process flows for these modules to help understand the areas susceptible to fraud.

Understanding the methods used for concealing fraud is also helpful. The 2018 RTTN reported that 55% of fraudsters created fraudulent physical documents, 48% altered physical documents and 42% created fraudulent transactions in the accounting system.

The longer perpetrators go undetected, the more financial harm they can cause. The good news is that 27% of cases are discovered in the first six months and the median duration of a fraud is 16 months.

Internal controls in companies cannot prevent fraud but they can detect and deter. The top three anti-fraud controls in companies are:

1. Code of conduct (80%)

2. External Audit of Financial Statements (80%)

3. Internal audit department (73%)

The 2018 RTTN discovered only 63% of victim organisations employ hotlines even though tips are the most common method of detecting fraud.

What internal factors should we consider for fraud risk assessments?

The lack of monitoring activities and inadequate controls contribute to the probability of fraud and embezzlement.

1. Management and/or Human Resources (HR) do not clearly define job roles, accountability, duties, and responsibilities. They may not provide advice to rectify and/ or fail to act upon substandard levels of job performance or problematic unethical behaviour.

2. Organisations do not communicate its mission statement, which is a formal summary of the aims and values of the company, to all employees. Values can include the importance of ethical behaviour and honesty.

3. Company employee policies do not address employee fraud or the consequences of committing acts of fraud.

4. There are irregular external and internal audits to ensure compliance with the company's policies and regulatory reporting requirements.

5. There is no employee hotline for reporting suspected fraud.

6. The company lacks on-line training programs on legal, ethical, fraud detection and security-related training.

We learned in Chapter 3 (Psychology of a Fraudster) that there are many reasons why people commit fraud. These include the following:

a. They think they can get away with it and employees rarely face long prison sentences for white collar crime. In addition, the organisation they work for has no history of punishing or prosecuting people so there is no deterrent.

b. The rewards of indulging in criminal behaviour may exceed the risk of detection and apprehension.

c. They believe they need the stolen money or objects.

d. They are frustrated or dissatisfied with their job, the organisation or company management and want revenge.

e. Internal controls are very weak, and their bosses and co-workers are corrupt, so it makes it easier to steal or cheat.

f. The employee is lazy or is in financial difficulty and thinks it is easier to steal from the organisation than to get a second job or ask for a company loan.

g. The employee is a compulsive thief.

h. In the case of market downturn and the company facing financial challenges, these factors may influence a senior executive to commit fraud such as knowingly inflating sales.

What is 'Inherent Risk'?

Inherent Risk exists in something as a permanent, essential or characteristic attribute, and is the risk an activity can pose if no controls or other mitigating factors are in place. For example, if we look at inherent risk in financial accounting, there is an inherent risk that we could misstate the financial statements due to the incorrect booking of accounting transactions especially if there are no controls in place. If we look at a retail business, there is an inherent risk that the theft of goods will occur as retail stores purchase sizable items of stock. Effective inventory management is particularly important, and many businesses install in-store security cameras to monitor employees and customers.

What is 'Residual Risk'?

Residual risk is the risk remaining after all controls and mitigating factors are taken into consideration. We can calculate the residual risk by subtracting controls from the inherent risk. In the 'Risk Assessment and Treatment' textbook from the Insurance Institute of America, residual risk is the risk remaining after altering the risk's likelihood or impact. Companies often assess the residual risk in terms of whether it leads to a tolerable level of residual risk. If the level of residual risk is unacceptable, the company will select and implement a risk treatment option such as buying insurance to further reduce the risk.

Traditionally we perceive risk as something negative, which we call pure risk as there is a chance of loss or no loss, but no chance of gain. Speculative risk can result in both negative and positive consequences.

Let us look at hedging, which is a method used by companies to manage foreign exchange risk. For example, if a company purchases goods in a foreign currency and the cost is EUR10,000 and at the prevailing EUR/USD exchange rate, it will cost the company USD12,000. The company plans to pay for the goods in two months' time, but they do not want to retain the risk of a fluctuation in the exchange rate leading to the price increasing in USD. The company can buy Euro from its bank at the current foreign exchange rate. However, it is also forgoing any profit if there is a favourable movement in the exchange rate. This is an example of a risk treatment choice that eliminates any risk of foreign exchange losses. In today's world, there are many financial instruments to help companies lower its residual risk exposure which appeals to risk adverse companies.

What should we consider when we prepare a fraud risk assessment checklist for a retail grocery business?

We suggest that every entity should conduct a formal risk assessment every 12 to 24 months.

Risk Factors	Control Reference
Opportunity to commit fraud: has the employer assessed and agreed the maximum amount in which employees might defraud the organization?, for example what is the limit that the cashier can refund to customers without management approval or does management need to approve all refunds? What is the cheque signing authority for individuals in the accounting department, do all cheques need a co-signature?	Accounting Policy Manual and Guidelines. Written Communication from the company on its cheque signing authority to its banks and/or other financial institutions.
Special relationships: Are management aware of any unique relationships between employees or between employees and suppliers that could lead to collusion and place the business at risk of collapse? If such relationships with suppliers and employees exist, do the owners and/or management of the business control the business interaction between the employee and the supplier? In the case of close employee relationships, do management rotate employee hours so they work different shifts? Most companies have strict policies on the value of gifts and benefits that vendors offer employees; the HR department and the CEO maintain gift registries.	HR addresses potentially close relationships between co-workers and vendors in initial and subsequent hiring interviews and discusses this subject thereafter in regular meetings with employees. HR records an Employee Gift Register and senior management review it quarterly and annually.

Risk Factors	Control Reference
Employee handbooks: Many organisations issue employee handbooks that employees review and sign on an annual basis. Do these policies address the company's discipline process for theft, for example, the company may suspend employees suspected of fraud while the company investigates the suspected theft, or they would dismiss the employee immediately if they committed a theft. Does the policy mention the involvement of law enforcement if the employee commits stealing? The company should also be mindful of potential for lawsuits such as discrimination or wrongful discharge if they follow through with a discharge with a protected class of employee or those who are on disability, pregnant or ill.	The Legal department records Employee Handbooks and Policy Manuals signed by each employee and communicates compliance to HR.
Controls: A company is more exposed to fraud if they have no or weak internal controls than those with tight documented controls. Examples of controls include segregation of duties, peer or management reviews and control checklists completed by employees when they carry out tasks, duties and responsibilities.	Department heads record and review completed control checklists on a weekly, monthly, and/or quarterly basis. Management conducts reviews of said checklists semi-annually and annually for each department.

Risk Factors	Control Reference
The lack of trust between management and employees and even between co-workers can cause a lot of angst in any company. In some cases, micromanaging undermines an employee's ability, and this usually leads to frustration and anger and as we discussed earlier, people commit fraud for revenge purposes.	No control available as this risk is based on relationships and we cannot measure meaningfully.
When management appear to lack ethical values: we learned that one of the main reasons for white-collar crimes is due to corrupt bosses setting a bad example for employees, making them more likely to steal or cheat.	No control available as this risk is difficult to measure.
Moral behaviour and minimizing the motivation to commit fraud: the owners/management of the company should exhibit their ethical and honest beliefs. Senior personnel have a duty to communicate the importance of ethical and honest dealings in day to day business of the company so middle management and employees are aware that this is a crucial element of the company's culture.	Regular communication of Mission Statement and adherence to Ethical values via web-based training and compliance courses.

Risk Factors	Control Reference
Training programs: Does the company have ethical and security training courses for new and existing employees? Many companies have mandatory training programs for new hires and all existing employees. These web-based programs often offer examples of what the company views as proper behaviour and a question and answer session at the end proves that the employee understands the company's position on these values.	The IT department records if each employee completes all mandatory internal web-based training programs and they communicates compliance to HR and senior management.
Hiring process: Is the company's hiring process documented with background checks including police records, professional organisation membership, pre-employment drug tests and two or more reference checks from previous employers? Nowadays, companies want employees to fit in with the company and soft skills are increasingly more important. Several companies often require employees to undertake pre-employment personality assessments.	HR employee hiring process checklist.

Risk Factors	Control Reference
Does the company provide employee assistance programs (EAPs)? These are common employee benefits in companies today, the program assists employees with personal problems and/or work-related problems that impact their work performance, health, mental and emotional wellbeing. This is mutually beneficial to the employee and the company as the employee can receive free professional advice and assistance usually in the form of counselling from the program anonymously as the company only receives statistics on employee usage.	Annual contract with an EAP company and HR records the annual statistics report from the EAP organisation.
Does the company offer attractive compensation packages including fringe benefits and opportunities for professional advancement and growth within the company? Is it competitive with other companies in the industry?	HR conducts annual salary reviews of peer companies. HR records all training programs completed by employees
Management awareness are management tuned into their employees' lifestyles and of any recently acquired wealth?	Regular team meetings and bi-monthly social events for informal interactions with all employees.
Physical access to the building	Only designated employees have keys. All entrances and exits are locked at close of business and alarm systems are activated.

Risk Factors	Control Reference
Control over physical access to high value products.	Management store alcohol and cigarettes in locked cabinets. Only management can access these products.
Control over physical access to cash.	Management lock their offices when unoccupied. Management makes daily cash deposits to its bank. Cameras are placed above all cash registers to deter employee theft.
Control over employee records including compensation and benefits details.	The HR department stores all employee records securely in its offices and access is limited to HR personnel and senior management only.

Risk Factors	Control Reference
Account reconciliations and financial reporting	The accounting department conducts monthly bank accounts reconciliations for all bank accounts. Aging of accounts receivable and accounts payable are performed monthly. Management receives monthly management reports including P&L and Balance Sheets. The accounting department prepares and explains variances for actual results for the month versus the same month last year and prepares variance analysis for year to date results versus prior year to date. The accounts department performs actual to budget variance analysis for management review. They also provide ratio analysis.
Annual **Stock taking**	Normally conducted in February by an external company and they communicate this information to the accounting department. The accounting department investigates large variances from this information to the closing stock numbers in the accounting system and present explanations to senior management.
Annual external financial **audit**	Per agreement with external audit firm.

In summary, fraud risk assessment is a continuous activity requiring management to constantly watch and adapt to the fraud environment and refresh the organisation's processes regularly.

If you don't invest in risk management, it doesn't matter what business you're in, it's a risky business.
Gary Cohn (Economist, philanthropist, and venture capital investor)

Chapter 10

Fraud Prevention

What are the main differences between policies and procedures?

A policy is an organisation's guiding principle to give direction to employees. Policies are clear, simple statements of how the organisation intends to conduct its services, actions or business. A company's accounting policy usually includes preferred accounting rules, an example being its preferred depreciation approach. When a company buys an asset, depreciation is the process of distributing the cost of the asset over its useful life, rather than deducting the full cost as an expense in the month or year of purchase.

The depreciation policy will recommend the minimum cost of the asset to be capitalised and depreciated. For example, all fixed assets purchased with a value of $5,000 or more should be capitalised and depreciated. The policy will also offer guidance on the preferred method and length of time for depreciation. For example, most companies depreciate its computer fixed assets, both hardware and software using a straight-line method over a three-year period.

Procedures describe how the organisation will implement each policy in the organisation. Each procedure should outline:

- Who performs which task?
- What steps to take.
- Which forms or documents to use.

An example of a procedure is when a staff member in the accounting department records the monthly computer depreciation amount in the general ledger. The staff accountant will use the fixed asset register spreadsheet to obtain the depreciation amount for the current month. The register records the date of purchase and cost of the asset, the length of the depreciation period and the monthly depreciation amount. The register will also have the Net Book Value of the asset at the end of each month, the net book value is the original cost of the asset less the accumulated depreciation.

The staff accountant will ask his/her supervisor to review the depreciation charge. Upon sign off, the staff accountant will enter the journal in the accounting system. Once recorded, the staff accountant will run an income statement and balance sheet report from the accounting system and reconcile the depreciation number and the net book value to the amount in the fixed asset register.

What techniques can we use to help increase the perception for detection

Perception of detection is one of the leading elements in fraud prevention. Preventing fraud is less costly than trying to recover losses.

Many potential fraudsters will contemplate actions several times before committing a fraud and evaluate whether it is worth the risk or not. The fraudster will contemplate the fear of punishment, imprisonment, humiliation and the loss of personal relationships. Techniques for increasing the perception of detection include:

- Surveillance
- Tips
- Surprise Audits
- Prosecution
- Enforcement of ethics and fraud policies
- Catching the fraudster

A company usually installs surveillance cameras in places where assets are subject to elevated risk of theft such as mailrooms where employees open envelopes containing cash and cheques, or above a teller's desk in a bank branch. It is not enough to install the cameras. Management should inform all staff they have installed cameras, so the staff are aware their activities are being watched.

According to the 2018 RTTN, tips are the most common detection method for organisational fraud. 53% of employees provide tips, followed by customers (21%), anonymous (14%) and vendors (8%). Many companies supply a link to an online reporting tool on its website for anyone who wishes to report an incident.

To complete the incident report, the individual usually needs to complete the following information:

- Issue Details and Involved Parties.
- Issue Date and Location.
- Photos or file uploads.
- The individual can also choose to remain anonymous and if he/she wishes to disclose his/her relationship to the organisation.

Companies often offer 24-hour telephone hotlines managed by live operators. These trained and experienced hotline operators fully debrief callers and ask pointed questions.

Fraudulent employees expect regular audits and cover their tracks accordingly. They can prepare deceptive answers for the auditors. A surprise audit can uncover a fraud and even the threat of a potential surprise audit can deter fraudulent behaviour. Surprise audits are one of the least-used forms of anti-fraud controls, but one of the most effective. According to the 2018 RTTN, only 37% percent of victim companies used surprise audits as a method of detection.

Prosecuting thieves to the fullest extent of the law sends a strong message that the company will punish those who commit financial crimes. In September 2014, the 82nd United States Attorney General, Mr. Eric Holder, gave a speech at NYU and emphasised the importance of identifying the company decision-makers who ought to be held criminally responsible because prosecution of such individuals "enhances accountability", "promotes fairness", and "has a powerful deterrent effect". Mr. Holder observed that "few things discourage criminal activity at a firm – or incentivise changes in corporate behaviour – like the prospect of individual decision-makers being held accountable".

According to the 2018 RTTN, the percentage of cases referred to law enforcement declined from 65% in 2012 to 58% in 2018 and the main reason for this was fear of bad publicity (38%) followed by internal discipline being sufficient (33%).

Why is it important for a company to enforce its ethics and fraud policies?

An organisation should have a clear plan of action if a fraud occurs including the penalties for various kinds and levels of fraud. It is best practice to establish the penalties before a fraud occurs and imposing the punishment is particularly important. Adherence to the company's anti-fraud policy has the same effect on the perception of detection as that of prosecution and surprise audits.

The greatest perception of detection is catching the fraudster, prosecuting him/her according to the law and publicising the treatment of the fraudster. An organisation communicates its policy of zero tolerance for fraud when it not only detects the fraud, but also prosecutes those who commit fraud. The company should also reward those who help detect fraud.

How does internal audit help in fraud detection?

In the 2018 RTTN, the initial detection of occupational frauds shows tips were the most common detection method by a wide margin, accounting for 40% of cases, internal audit (15%) edged out management review (13%) as the second and third most common detection method respectively.

Internal audits create a strong feeling of detection and can therefore serve as a preventative measure. The internal audit function periodically verifies the legitimacy of transactions and confirms the entity's assets exist.

Accounting controls are set up to detect any fraud which may occur in between periodic audits. Finding, reviewing and analysing abnormalities are important if regular audits are to be effective.

Studies have found that organisations with an internal audit function are more likely than those without such a function to detect fraud within its organisation. The internal audit department should have adequate resources and authority to run effectively and without undue influence from senior management.

When planning an internal audit, the auditor should assess fraud and error risks as these can lead to significant misrepresentations in the financial reports and the auditor should request information from management about any substantial fraud or error they discovered. The auditor should seek sufficient and appropriate proof that fraud and error was not committed or if there is an existence of fraud and error, then if the impact was reflected in the financial statements, and if and when the error was corrected.

What is the commanding approach in fraud detection?

As discussed earlier, top management sets the tone at the top for the rest of the organisation. An organisation's culture plays a vital role in preventing, detecting and deterring fraud. Management is responsible for creating a culture through words and actions that clearly communicate that the company will not tolerate fraud, and that any such behaviour will be dealt with swiftly and decisively, and whistle-blowers will not suffer retribution.

The commanding approach, also known as the directive approach, comes from the top of the organisation. This approach is confrontational, authoritative and firm. This approach clearly states that if someone commits a fraud, he/she will be discovered and fired. In this case, the organisation does not so much take steps to prevent fraud but if someone steals, he/she will simply lose his/her job. Management are often surprised to learn that employees have committed acts of fraud.

What is the difference between Precautionary Approach and Detective Approach?

Precautionary Approach

Proactive and preventative measures are the best way to reduce fraud in the workplace. Human Resources should conduct police background checks on potential new hires and in some cases, require pre-employment drugs tests. Once the person is employed, he/she ought to follow policies and procedures, and conduct tasks that require peer reviews. Segregation of duties and mandatory vacation time for employees also helps prevent fraud and error. An example of segregation of duties include requiring two signatures on all cheques. Another example is the person who reconciles the bank statement for the company's bank accounts should be a different individual to the person signing cheques, and also be a separate individual to the person recording transactions in the company's general ledger system.

Detective Approach

This entails setting up strong accounting controls and an internal audit function to watch transactions against potential frauds. The internal audit function is to periodically verify the legitimacy of transactions and confirming the company's assets exist. For example, in the instance of a property insurance underwriter alerting the accounting department to increase the annual estimated premium income from a client from $2.5 million to $3.0 million (a 20% increase) based on additions to the underlying coverage.

In this instance, an internal auditor should investigate the transaction and review all email correspondence and premium receipts received from the client to determine if it is indeed correct to increase the estimated premium. The internal audit team wants to prevent the underwriter from receiving a larger bonus based on fictitious numbers. The internal audit team should also confirm with the accounting department if it recorded and collected all expected cash receipts from this client. This is an illustration of internal audit periodically verifying transactions and confirming the company's cash assets exist.

How are these approaches used for fraud detection?

In the precautionary approach, background police checks can raise red flags and establish if the potential employee has a history of or is inclined to commit fraud. A pre-employment drugs test can alert the employer to the fact that financial pressure may exist for the potential employee to support his/her drug habit. A positive drug test also begs the question if the candidate can actual fulfil his/her duties. According to the 2018 RTTN, only 4% of fraudsters had prior convictions for a fraud related offence. Employers should always follow up on employment references as they may uncover background information that went unnoticed during the recruitment process.

In the detective approach, internal audit identifying, reviewing, and analysing irregularities are important for effective audits. According to the 2018 RTTN, internal audit came in second after tips as the most common detection method. This was across all regions except for the United States and Western Europe, where management review came in second. Whilst internal audits are detective in nature, they can also function as a preventive measure. The very absence of an internal audit function can lead to an increase in fraud related activities.

What are 'Internal Controls' and what examples of internal control activities can organisations adopt to help prevent fraud activities?

Internal Controls are methods established by a company to ensure the integrity of financial and accounting information, to meet operational and profitability targets, and to transmit management policies throughout its organisation.

I like the definition provided by www.businessdictionary.com. It states that internal controls are systematic measures (such as reviews, checks and balances, methods and procedures) instituted by an organisation to:

1. Conduct its business in an orderly and efficient manner.

2. Safeguard its assets and resources.

3. Deter and detect errors, fraud, and theft.

4. Ensure accuracy and completeness of its accounting data.

5. Produce reliable and timely financial and management information.

6. Ensure adherence to its policies and plans.

Internal controls can influence the opportunity to commit fraud. The following are internal control activities that might serve as preventative measures.

Adequate Authorisation Procedures: This often means that cheques require two signatories or a person who enters a vendor in the computer system cannot authorise the vendor but requires separate approval by another individual.

Adequate Documentation, Records and Audit Trail: An example of this is all vendors require a valid and authorised invoice to receive payment and organisations require all receipts from employees for expense reimbursements.

Physical Control Over Assets and Records: Physical control over assets and records helps protect an organisation's assets. Physical precautions include security guards, locked doors, fireproof vaults and password verification to access computers and printers. Another control is storing daily, weekly and monthly back-up copies of computerised records at reputable off-site companies.

Independent Performance Checks: Employees who did not perform the tasks will carry out these checks (also known as peer or supervisory review). These reviews can identify errors, procedural deficiencies and/or staff incompetence. Routine checks normally take place after completion of tasks and/or transactions.

Monitoring of Controls: Research has shown that unmonitored controls tend to weaken over time. Control monitoring can help the organisation to:

- Promptly identify and correct internal control problems.

- Produce more accurate and reliable information for decision-making.

- Prepare exact and timely financial statements.

- Provide periodic certifications or assertions on the effectiveness of internal controls.

Over time effective monitoring can lead to organisational efficiencies and reduced costs because we can find problems and address them in an initiative-taking, rather than a reactive manner.

What important points should we consider when developing a fraud policy?

We should develop a fraud policy before a theft occurs. There are several issues to consider:

A definition of actions we deem to be fraudulent. Examples of fraud includes activities such as theft, corruption, conspiracy, embezzlement, money laundering, bribery, and extortion.

A statement from the CEO/Owner to management and employees informing them that the company will take all measures to deter fraud. The company should also provide the appropriate fraud and corruption training or guidance to employees. All employees should read and sign the fraud policy upon commencing employment with the company and thereafter on an annual basis. They should receive email alerts when the policy is updated so they can review the changes and/or additions to the policy.

The method management will adopt when they detect or suspect irregularities. Managers should immediately report suspected misconduct or dishonesty to his/her superior, internal audit, legal department or other department as stipulated in the fraud policy.

The formal procedure employees should take if they suspect a fraud and encouragement or incentives for all employees to report any suspicion of fraud. The fraud policy should ensure it protects the person reporting the fraud or suspected fraud and his/her identity should remain confidential.

Notification to management and employees that the company will investigate all instances of suspected fraud. It will report actual frauds to the appropriate authorities, and it will prosecute all guilty offenders.

A statement that the company will exert all efforts to recover wrongfully obtained assets from thieves. Recovery is always difficult as fraudsters usually spend the money they steal.

In terms of recovery of losses, the 2018 RTTN pointed out the more victims lose to organisational fraud, the less likely they are likely to make a full recovery. The statistics are quite gloomy.

Amount Lost	Percent recovered
Less than $10,000	30%
$10,000 to $100,000	16%
$100,001 to $1,000,000	13%
$1,000,000+	8%

The good news is that experience has shown that the most effective and reliable approach to achieving full recovery is through business insurance. Whilst some insurance providers simply pay the loss to the company without an investigation, the best response usually involves an adequate insurance plan together with aggressive litigation to obtain full recovery.

If you forgive the fox for stealing your chickens, he will take your sheep.
Georgian Proverb

Chapter 11

Computer Crimes

What are Computer Forensics?

Computer forensics are a subdivision of digital forensic science and relates to evidence stored on computers and digital storage media. The goal of computer forensics is to examine digital media in a forensically sound manner with the aim of identifying, preserving, recovering, analysing and presenting facts and opinions about the digital information.

Computer forensics are used in criminal and civil proceedings.

Computers may constitute the 'scene of a crime', for example in cases of hacking, denial of service attacks or they may hold evidence in the form of emails, internet history, documents or other files relevant to fraud crimes.

Systems and data are powerful tools in preventing, detecting, and investigating fraud; therefore, technology plays a significant role in the fraud environment.

It is not just the content of emails, documents and other files which may be of interest to investigators but also the 'metadata' associated with those files. In Chapter 6, we discussed metadata as data that describe data. The metadata of a bank record is the information related to transactions. This information includes date, time, teller information, origin and the format of the transaction. Investigators may find numerous clues in metadata and a computer forensic examination may reveal when a document first appeared on a computer, when it was last edited, saved or printed and which user carried out these actions.

Today with the vast increase in individuals using social media, we need to be more aware and security conscious about what we share online to minimise the threat of fraud such as identity theft and credit/debit card fraud.

Why do we conduct computer forensic engagements?

A variety of sources may request computer forensic assistance including corporate security professionals, internal and external audit teams, in-house counsel, outside law firms, and those with authority investigating civil or criminal fraudulent cases such as law enforcement personnel. Potential computer forensic engagements can encompass fraud prevention and detection control assessments, bankruptcy-related investigations, dispute advisory assistance, and investigations which include financial reporting and security investigations, regulatory compliance investigations, and misappropriation of assets amongst others.

What sources can assist us in retrieving data?

Forensic data may exist in any device with data storage such as:

- PCs and laptop computers - documents and working papers saved to hard drives.
- Back up tapes.
- Solid state storage (SSS) – stores data electronically instead of magnetically.

- Removable disks – for example a SD card and memory card reader.

- Thumb drives such as a USB stick.

- IP telephone systems keeps records of incoming and outgoing calls and voicemails.

- Highly capable smartphones and Personal Digital Assistants.

- E-mail – on company servers or those archived and stored remotely.

- Faxes stored on network drives.

- All-in-one printers (also known as a printer scanner copier or PSC): In today's working environment, PSCs can track an individual's copying, scanning and printing activities. Many organisations require users to log in to these PSCs to access copy and print material and to scan documents. The company network often stores copies on its network.

- Recycle bins.

- Instant messages: Some business instant messaging software tools offer a record keeping function to save and archive correspondence to retrieve as a reference whenever required.

- Mainframes and servers.

- Data stored on the 'cloud'.

What are the characteristics of a computer forensic analysis?

A systematic computer forensic analysis has the following characteristics:

- Ability to apply sound and replicable methodologies. Methodologies are replicable when another person can repeat a process and obtain the same results.

- Using practices that have withstood challenges in the past. The expert should have the necessary qualifications and licences to provide sound advice.

- Comprehensive documentation, as discussed in previous chapters, documenting evidence is an important focus of a forensic accounting investigation.

- Using software, which is acceptable in the forensic profession, there is Basic Productivity Software such as Microsoft Excel and Microsoft Access. There are also Add-On data analysis software packages that leverage Excel to perform data analysis. Forensic accountants also use data analysis software such as IDEA and ACL and special purpose software to facilitate advanced data analyses.

What are the benefits of data analysis?

If a forensic accountant needs to manually analyse thousands of line items, for example journal entries, invoices and disbursements, it can be tedious and time-consuming and a task prone to error. With the help of sophisticated and powerful software, the forensic accountant can analyse 100% of the data. The company's general ledger, sales database and time and expense systems can all be sources for the data that needs analysing as well as user files, network drives and web logs. Examples of sources of data software packages include Adobe Acrobat, email systems, Microsoft Office products like Excel, Word, PowerPoint and ERP systems such as SAP and PeopleSoft.

ERP systems stand for Enterprise Resource Planning system and they incorporate most or all features of an organisation. For example, PeopleSoft has different modules such as accounts payable, treasury and general ledger amongst others. The data from accounts payable interfaces directly with the general ledger and ERP systems can eliminate and reduce the risk of interfacing data from separate systems. Medium-sized and large-size companies normally use these products, as they are usually too expensive to purchase and maintain for small companies.

The benefits of using data analysis include:

- Reducing and even eradicating sampling risk. Sampling risk is the risk of the sample data analysed by an auditor being vastly different to the results if he/she analysed 100% of the data.

- We can compare relevant data from various sources and systems to gain a broader view of the data.

- We can monitor and analyse data trends including fluctuating trends and quickly identify potential risk factors and false positives. A false positive is a result that indicates that a given condition exists when in fact it does not. We can inform the company and personnel of any anomalies that we identify, and we can extract certain risk criteria from the entire population for further analysis.

- We can test the usefulness of the company's internal controls, procedures and policies.

What legal factors should we consider before starting computer forensic engagements?

Forensic teams should contemplate the following legal factors before embarking on an engagement:

Subpoenas

Is there a subpoena that allows for collection of data? A subpoena is a writ for the summoning of witnesses or the submission of evidence, such as records or documents before a court.

There are two common types of subpoenas:

- *Subpoena Ad Testificandum* orders a person to provide oral testimony before an ordering authority or face punishment. Subpoenas can request the testimony to be given by phone or in person.

- *Subpoena Duces Tecum* orders a person or organisation to bring physical evidence before the ordering authority or face punishment. These pertain for requests to provide copies of documents or evidence to the requesting party or directly to court.

Regarding the collection of data, the second mentioned subpoena, Subpoena Duces Tecum is applicable.

Qualifications

Is the forensic accountant qualified? Is it mandatory for the forensic accountant to hold a recognised licence?

Can the forensic team employ unqualified people to collect or analyse the data or can they only employ licensed private investigators?

Do the forensic accountants have the legal authority to access the data and produce evidence? Do the engagement team have legal advice available to them?

Privacy Laws

In cases of international data collection, is the engagement team aware of the laws about international privacy? I researched a number of websites and learned that Information Privacy or data protection laws prohibit the disclosure or misuse of information about private individuals. Over 80 countries and independent territories, including nearly every country in Europe and many in Latin America and the Caribbean, Asia, and Africa, have now adopted comprehensive data protection laws. The OECD published Guidelines on the Protection of Privacy and Trans-border Flows of Personal Data. The European Data Protection Directive protects the collection, use and disclosure of personal information held by the private and public sector. The European Union (EU) adopted this Directive and all member states of the EU have enacted their own data protection legislation. Every year, the International Conference of Data Protection and Privacy Commissioners brings together the highest authorities and institutions guaranteeing data protection and privacy, as well as experts in the field from every continent.

Conflicts of interest

Does the team know to whom the data belong, and are there any privacy concerns? Is there any conflict of interest? Conflicts of interest can possibly influence decision making. A conflict of interest is a risk that professional judgement or actions regarding a primary interest will be unduly influenced by a secondary interest. If there is a potential conflict of interest with an individual within the team, the individual cannot normally participate in the investigation.

Law enforcement involvement

Does the team expect to find data, such as those related to national security issues or child pornography, which they need to report to law enforcement authorities? There are many websites available to report child pornography, including https://www.asacp.org the Association of Sites Advocating Child Protection (ASACP), which is a non-profit organisation dedicated to eliminating child exploitation from the Internet. There is also a site to report national security issues, https://www.gov.uk/government/organisations/national-security. Even though these websites exist, I think it is prudent from the start of the investigation to alert a member(s) of the police force and/or other law enforcement agencies if the team expects to uncover such data. This also ensures the investigation team is aware of the protocol or process to follow. They should have a contact person and a qualified member of law enforcement to aid them if they discover anything inappropriate or troubling. This also helps the team to build a relationship with law enforcement agencies.

What tools do forensic accountants use for data analysis?

The following software tools are often employed by those conducting data analyses:

- Many accountants and corporate employees have encountered Excel during their career. Excel is a spreadsheet application developed by Microsoft. Its basic feature is calculation and it is also a powerful tool for analysing data especially the pivot table feature. A typical pivot table summarises and organises data from spreadsheet data into a table. From the pivot table, the user can sort, filter and analyse the data from multiple perspectives. This is a splendid feature as different individuals can slice and dice the information for their unique needs without editing or corrupting the underlying data. Microsoft also offers many add-on programs such as Analysis ToolPak that provides data analytic tools for financial, statistical and engineering data analyses. ActiveData add-in for Excel converts substantial amounts of data in a company's records into manageable databases, which individuals can then query and summarise according to their preference

- According to https://www.audimation.com/Product-Detail/CaseWare-IDEA, IDEA is a powerful and user-friendly tool designed to help accounting and financial professionals extend their auditing capabilities, detect fraud and meet documentation standards. It easily imports data from almost any source to analyse large data sets, report findings using visualisation tools and automate repeatable processes without programming. The promotional video highlights that a user can:

- Analyse data faster.

- Identify control breakdowns.

- Improve its audits.

- IDEA seems to be a sound software package as you can use it even if you are unfamiliar with the data under analysis.

- ACL has many audit and accounting solutions. According to its website, https://www.acl.com/solutions/fraud-management/ companies and government agencies use this Fraud Management software. They use ACL for a 360° anti-fraud solution combining prevention and detection to shake down suspicious activities.

It is important to note that all users of these software programs should only obtain read-only access to the data to prevent editing and to preserve the integrity of the data.

What type of information is contained in a chain of custody form?

We discussed the importance of a Chain of Custody in previous chapters. The investigation team needs to safeguard this evidence so the suspect or suspects do not destroy it and they should always observe the chain of custody when gathering evidence. If the investigative team does not follow the chain of custody, a court of law may challenge the evidence and even consider it inadmissible.

A chain of custody must prove that individuals did not have the opportunity to tamper with the evidence. It is crucial to keep a detailed log as to who had personal custody of the evidence at any given time. Without a documented chain of custody, it is almost impossible to prove that nobody tampered with the evidence. In addition, a court judge may rule the evidence inadmissible in his/ her court room due to possible interference by an individual or group of individuals. In turn, this may be a prominent concern in the context of a criminal prosecution as we must prove the accused is guilty 'beyond reasonable doubt'.

An identifiable person should always have the physical custody of a piece of evidence. In practice, this means a police officer or detective will take charge of a piece of evidence, document its collection and hand it over to an evidence clerk for storage in a secure place. The chain of custody requires us to document the transfer of said evidence from person to person and prove that nobody else accessed the evidence. It is best to keep the number of transfers of evidence as low as possible.

A typical computer chain of evidence provides three sections, one for the original collector to complete, the second deals with copy history and the third section addresses transfer history.

The first section filled out by the initial collector includes information on:

- Who collected the evidence?
- Date and time of collection.
- Description of the collection method.

- The application software/utility required to view the file.
- Where was the evidence initially stored?
- How was the evidence initially secured?
- Collector signature and date.

The second section is for copy history and includes columns for:

- Date.
- Copied by.
- Copy method.
- Disposition of original and all copies.

The Transfer History section requires the following information to record every transfer of evidence from person to person:

- Date and time.
- Transferred from (print name, sign & date).
- Transferred to (print name, sign & date).
- Where is the evidence stored?
- How is the evidence secured?

It is vital that once we establish the chain of custody, we as a team needs to preserve it to avoid lapses in protocol, which may affect the credibility of our entire examination.

Data will talk to you if you are willing to listen.

Jim Bergeson

Chapter 12

Working in a Forensic Team

What does an internal auditor do?

It is important for forensic accountants to work well with both internal and external auditors. Both sets of auditors are very different. The internal auditor is usually comprised of individuals employed by the organisation who work on a full-time basis to review the operational activities of an organisation, whereas external auditors are an external accounting firm that perform an audit and provides its opinion on the financial statements of the company. The management of the organisation appoints the internal auditors and determines the scope of work. If the board of directors appoint an audit committee, this committee are ultimately responsible for the oversight of the internal audit team. Internal audit teams often conduct risk assessments which they should perform to IIA standards, which means International Standards for the Professional Practice of Internal Auditing (Standards). The Standards are principle-focused and provide a framework for performing and promoting internal auditing.

The Standards are mandatory requirements consisting of:

- Statements of basic requirements for the professional practice of internal auditing and for evaluating the effectiveness of its performance. The requirements are internationally applicable at organisational and individual levels.

- Interpretations, which clarify terms or concepts within the statements.
- Glossary terms.

It is necessary to consider both the statements and their interpretations to understand and apply the Standards correctly. The Standards employ terms that have specific meanings as noted in the Glossary, which is also part of the Standards.

The goal of internal auditors is to review the routine operational activities of an organisation and recommend improvements. This often involves site visits by internal audit personnel.

The internal auditors also evaluate accounting and controls systems, analyse financial and non-financial information of the company, and detect any errors or misstatements in the financial statements.

Internal auditors often identify key controls within the company's departments and are usually ultimately responsible for documenting these controls. They provide the individual departments with control checklists which they can refer to and complete and sign on monthly, quarterly and annual basis. To gain buy-in, the internal auditors normally work with the individual departments to develop these control checklists.

What are the goals of internal auditors in forensic investigations?

The internal audit team will be interested in co-operating with the management, completing the annual audit plan within the scheduled time period and shielding the internal audit team from criticism as it is very likely that the internal audit team will feel embarrassed about not detecting the fraud.

Even though internal audit may be ashamed about failing to discover the fraud, according to the 2018 RTTN, the initial detection rate of occupational fraud by internal audit is only 15%. It is the second most common detection method after tips, which is 40%.

The internal audit team will be interested in cooperating with management especially for damage control as the CEO will be concerned about the impact on the company's stock price, its brand, reputation, and employee morale. The CFO will be interested in the timeliness of the investigation and he/she will want it cleared up as soon as possible because he/she will likely be ashamed that it happened under his/her watch. The internal audit team will therefore provide as much information and complete any assigned tasks in a speedy but careful manner. Even though, the company's management will be concerned with costs, they will often hire temporary staff to assist the internal auditors.

If it is the end of the financial year, the internal audit team will be concerned with completing its annual audit of the financial statements within the appointed time period. If it is not year-end, the internal audit team will probably conduct an interim audit in conjunction with the external auditors.

How do forensic accountants collaborate with external auditors?

The external auditor may have a good working relationship with the company, or the relationship may be tense due to past events. It is usually in the company's best interests to have a good relationship with external auditors as they can provide sound and wise advice, especially as they may have prior experience which they can use to assist the company with any issues they may have. We should also remember that audit firms have many specialist employees; their knowledge and experience can be invaluable to the company. With the development of constant regulatory change and increased SEC scrutiny, the Board and the CFO often see the benefit of a collaborative relationship with external auditors and encourage a strong working relationship.

Due to the external auditors' experience with the company, they usually have a wealth of information which can be valuable to the forensic accountants including but not limited to the company's business process, documentation, systems and the areas of risk they already identified during their annual review or they have discussed with the audit committee and the Chief Risk Officer. The external auditors should welcome the opportunity to share this information with the forensic accountants and provide additional information in more informal verbal conversations.

The forensic team may need to obtain formal letters in order to gain access to the auditors' working papers which are documents that record all audit evidence obtained during financials statement audits and any other auditing work conducted by the audit firm. Working papers provide evidence that the auditors performed the audit per relevant auditing standards.

For example, the audit was:

- carefully planned

- conducted

- supervised

- appropriately reviewed

- the audit evidence is sufficient and appropriate to support the audit opinion

Unfortunately, obtaining formal access letters can take time and may delay the investigation.

What is the role of forensic accounting investigators when working in a forensic team?

One of the most important things for the forensic accountant investigators is to find facts. However, they are not encouraged to give opinions or reach conclusions.

Even though, the forensic accountants will follow direction by whomever hired them, they should ask the following questions to assess and assist in the investigation.

- **Who is involved?**

    Is it an executive, senior management, an employee or an external perpetrator, for example, a hacker? We learned in previous chapters and from the 2018 RTTN, that when owners or executives commit fraud, the median damage was USD$850,000. This is more than six times larger than when management were perpetrators as they stole an average of USD$150,000. The owners and executive's median loss was over seventeen times larger than the average loss caused by low-level employees, which amounted to USD$50,000.

Hacking is extremely common in today's world. The culprits are hard at work stealing records from companies which usually leads to financial losses for the company. In one case involving T.J. Maxx, hackers gained access to TJ Maxx's internal system and remained undetected for 18 to 24 months. They accessed 45.7 million credit card numbers. In 2007, business analysts estimated the rehabilitation costs of this data breach incident could cost the company USD$1 billion.

- **Is there a possibility that co-conspirators exist or did someone with a higher position in the organization instruct the perpetrator to commit the crime?**

If so, do we know the identity of this individual? Is he/she part of senior management? Are they aware of the investigation? Are they able to destroy or conceal evidence? As we learned in earlier chapters, it is easier for high-level managers and employees to steal because they usually can override and bypass internal controls easier as they are more familiar with the company's systems and internal controls, leading to their ability to steal money from the company. Research has shown that senior management steal large sums of money as opposed to lower-level employees who usually steal lesser amounts.

- **What is the magnitude of the crime and what is its impact on financial statements?**

According to the 2018 RTTN, the study analysed 2,690 occupational fraud cases that cost a total loss of more than $7 billion. The median loss of a fraud was $130,000 but 22% of occupational fraud cases resulted in a loss of at least $1million. The Board and the Management will be extremely interested to know the cost of the crime. If the fraud is public knowledge, then the company's creditors will be concerned about payment for goods and services, and the company's lenders will be concerned about repayment of any debt.

- **What was the time period over which the fraud occurred?**

The longer the perpetrators are undetected, the higher the losses tend to be. Again, from the 2018 RTTN, we learned that the average duration of a scheme was 16 months, but over two thirds of frauds last at least two years before detection. The median cost of frauds that went undetected for more than five years was $715,000.

- **Have we identified all material schemes?**

We learned earlier that asset misappropriation schemes account for the majority of fraud cases. In 2018 such schemes accounted for 89% of cases, these schemes tend to cause the lowest losses but there are numerous asset misappropriation sub-schemes such as cash theft, fraudulent disbursements, billing fraud, check tampering and misuse of assets. Corruption is in second place where purchasing and sales schemes are common. Then financial statement fraud which involves the overstating or understating the net worth and/or income of the Company. However, we learned that there can be overlapping schemes and the forensic accountant needs to be able to identify all these schemes.

- **How did the fraud happen?**

The forensic team should consider who found the fraud and how. They should also consider if it could have been detected earlier.

- **How can we avoid the recurrence of fraud?**

In Chapter 10 we discussed fraud prevention techniques and how organisations can adopt internal controls to prevent fraudulent activities and safeguard its assets and resources to help deter and detect errors, fraud, and theft. Internal controls also aid the organisation in conducting its business in an orderly and efficient manner and help provide reliable and timely financial information to management.

We also discussed that companies should consider internal control activities which include companies contemplating its authorisation procedures; for example, segregation of duties and requiring two signatories on invoice payments. Companies should also remember that adequate documentation and records such as expense reimbursement receipts help to deter fraud. All companies have physical assets and records. Some physical precautions such as locked doors, password verifications and security guards can help safeguard assets, as well as adequate backup copies of computerised records.

How do forensic accounting investigators collaborate with legal advisers?

Forensic accounting investigators should understand the following issues whilst working with legal personnel:

- The role and responsibilities of other team members involved in the investigation: the forensic accountant will be interested in the other team members' professions, fraud experience and skillsets.

- The degree to which the SEC, tax commissioners and any other external agencies which are involved or interested in fraud cases and the outcome of these cases. According to www.sec.gov, the agency specifically states that its mission is as follows: "The SEC is to protect investors; maintain fair, orderly, and efficient markets; and facilitate capital formation, the website also states that the SEC strives to promote a market environment that is worthy of the public's trust". SEC employees are committed to reviewing companies on an on-going basis. Companies should expect to receive regular requests for information if the SEC has questions regarding the company's financial statements or notes to its financial statements based on the company's quarterly and annual filings, namely 10-Q's and 10-K's.

- The legal aspects such as the extent of privilege, which protects all communication between the attorneys and the client from being disclosed to a third party, this encourages the client to disclose all information to his/her legal advisers. The forensic accountant should also be aware of the expected criminal charges. The Fraud Act 2006 is an Act of the Parliament of the United Kingdom, which asserts that a person found guilty of fraud is liable to imprisonment for up to twelve months on summary conviction and imprisonment for up to ten years upon conviction on indictment.

- Anticipated timing issues such as delays obtaining search warrants, access to public records, and as mentioned earlier, obtaining access letters to internal and external auditors working papers.

I would expect the forensic accountants to assist the legal team in the following areas:

1. Preparing, maintaining and distributing a working-group list of all parties to the investigation and the timing and nature of the expected interaction with these parties.

2. Preparing meeting schedules and agendas for meetings with the company's management and employees. Communicating the progress of the investigation to relevant parties.

3. In Chapter 6, we spoke about compiling, submitting and tracking various document and personnel access requests made by the investigating team. The amount of

documentation in a financial crime can be overwhelming and investigators need to collect vast amounts of information to support a conviction especially in complex financial crimes. It is important to assemble evidence in a well thought out and orderly fashion for all the paperwork accumulated throughout the investigation. We must try to avoid information overload, loss or destruction of the documents and a have a plan for storing the documents before we even begin to collect data.

4. Creating a chain of custody. The forensic investigator should discuss the level of detailed record-keeping with the client and legal counsel before gathering evidence. The evidence should be sufficiently useful to prove something important in a trial. As discussed in earlier chapters, an investigator needs to follow the chain of custody when gathering evidence, which is the movement and location of physical evidence from the time the investigator obtains the evidence until the time they present it in court. A well-organised assembly of evidence is a must to achieve this objective.

5. The forensic accountant should be familiar with the investigative process and have a sound understanding of accounting and auditing standards and procedures, as well as an understanding of GAAP/IFRS rules as they pertain to each investigation. Ideally, the forensic accountant should be able to read and understand financial statements.

6. The forensic accountant should be able to assess a

company's internal controls, policies and procedures, and identify potential weaknesses.

7. The forensic accountant should also be proficient in conducting background checks on individuals and on companies.

8. The forensic accountant should have knowledge of the investigative process and understand the importance of non-financial sources of evidence such as interviews, body language, statement analysis and handwriting analysis and be efficient in interpreting these sources of evidence.

What is the importance of privacy in forensic investigations? And, which measures can we take to achieve this?

As we discussed in earlier chapters, the 2018 RTTN discovered that asset misappropriation was by far the most common form of occupational fraud, occurring in 89% of cases, but causing the smallest median loss of $114,000. Financial statement fraud was on the other end of the spectrum, occurring in 10% of cases but causing a median loss of $800,000. Corruption cases fell in the middle, with 38% of cases and a median loss of $250,000. The schemes in the Financial Statement fraud category involve some form of falsified or manipulated financial statements. Investigations focus on financial statement fraud and if there are material misstatements, they need to inform the stakeholders. There is a risk that previously relied on financial statements could have been misstated as well and the investigators may need to detect past errors and report them to the company's senior management in order for them to correct these errors.

When a publicly traded company decides it needs to amend its financial statements, it must file SEC form 8-K within four days to notify investors of non-reliance on previously issued financial statements. It also needs to file amended 10-Q forms for the affected quarters and possibly amended 10-Ks, depending on how many accounting periods were affected by the erroneous data. In some cases, the SEC takes legal action against companies and individuals engaged in fraudulent financial reporting.

Whilst the company may need to disclose information to certain regulators, the company should be very wary of announcing any financial fraud publicly until it can identify the fraud schemes used and quantify the fiscal impact.

In earlier chapters, we spoke about the importance of confidentiality in cases where a company employee may be a suspect in a financial fraud and the investigation team needs time to communicate with third parties who may have access to or possess documentary evidence. These third parties include his/her financial institutions such as banks and insurance companies, professional service providers such as accountants, lawyers and investment advisers, industry contacts such as business associations, government officials and personal contacts. It is of utmost importance that the suspect is not aware that he/she is under investigation as he/she may abscond from the jurisdiction and/or destroy evidence that the investigation team has not yet uncovered. The investigators should discreetly familiarise themselves with the suspect's behavioural patterns regarding his/her personal and business activities in order to gain knowledge of the suspect in order to avoid making faulty judgements and/or missing and discarding important evidence.

To maintain confidentiality of the day-to-day developments in the investigation, it is important that the number of people who know about these developments is extremely limited. It is advisable for all personnel involved in the investigation to sign a Non-Disclosure Agreement (NDA), also known as a confidentiality agreement which is a legal contract between two parties that outlines confidential material, knowledge or information that the parties wish to share with one another for certain purposes but wish to restrict access to or by third parties. It is a contract through which the parties agree not to disclose information covered by the agreement. When drafted and used properly, confidentiality agreements are an effective way to protect confidential information.

We must also remember that many professional bodies have a code of ethics which their members usually review and agree to on an annual basis; most people abide by professional integrity, which is of utmost importance in legal investigations.

"Play fair, be prepared for others to play dirty, and don't let them drag you into the mud."

Sir Richard Branson (Businessman, investor, author and philanthropist)

Final Thoughts

The quest for justice and a fairer society for all is something we should all work towards. However there will always be greed, opportunists and vulnerable people to be scammed.

The *Reality of Greed* is meant to be used as a working tool and resource for fraud investigation and forensic accounting.

I hope that having read this comprehensive publication, your eyes have been opened even further and you feel equipped to meet the challenges that lie ahead in your role working in the field of financial and forensic fraud investigations.

Printed in Great Britain
by Amazon

75792540R00095